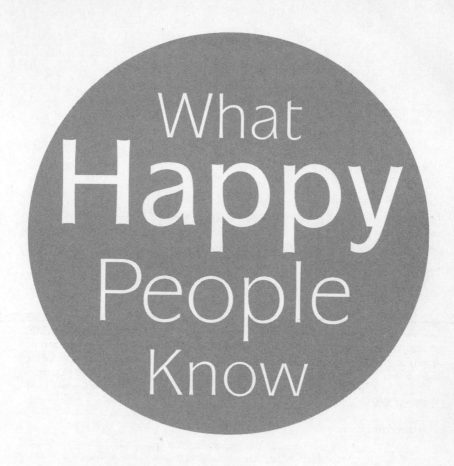

What Happy People Know

How the New Science of Happiness Can
Change Your Life for the Better

DAN BAKER, Ph.D.
Director of the Life Enhancement Program at Canyon Ranch
and CAMERON STAUTH

ST. MARTIN'S GRIFFIN ☒ NEW YORK

Notice

The stories shared in this book are about real people. All outcomes reported are true. However, great care has been taken to protect the actual identities of the people who were the inspiration for this book.

www.stmartins.com

Book design by Christina Gaugler

Library of Congress Cataloging-in-Publication Data

Baker, Dan.
    What happy people know : how the new science of happiness can change your life
for the better / Dan Baker and Cameron Stauth.
        p. cm.
    ISBN 1-57954-602-1 (hc)
    ISBN 0-312-32159-7 (pbk)
    1. Happiness. I. Stauth, Cameron. II. Title.
BF575.H27 B35 2002
158.1—dc21   2002014225

First published in the United States by Rodale

First St. Martin's Griffin Edition: January 2004

10 9 8 7 6 5 4 3 2 1

For my wife, Amy—my inspiration, grounding force, and love of my life. For my children—the manifestation of family, meaning, and purpose. For my grandchildren—the personification of possibilities and hope. And for my mother, whose nurturance and encouragement laid the foundation for a fulfilling and meaningful life.

Dan Baker

For Norm and Peggy Levine, poets of living.

Cameron Stauth

"Happiness is the whole aim and end of human existence."
Aristotle, *The Nicomachean Ethics*

Contents

Acknowledgments

The authors are sincerely grateful for the help of the following people.

Tammerly Booth, Editor-in-Chief of Women's Health Books at Rodale, who transformed a possibility into a reality

Mary South, skillful and astute editor, who helped make this book a reflection of her own talent and sensitivity

Richard Pine, creative force and guiding hand, who understood this book before it was written

Arthur Pine, a man of unconquerable optimism, whose living spirit is in these pages

Mel and Enid Zuckerman, for creating the incredible vision that is Canyon Ranch

Linda Richman, teacher beyond comparison and courageous confidante

Sandra Stahl, friend, advisor, and the first to see each chapter

Korri Fink, who adroitly researched this book until the recall to war of her husband, U.S. Marine Corps Scout Corporal Shane Fink

The guests of Canyon Ranch, an amazing group of people who live life to the fullest

Our families

And all of the people who have taught us that happiness is the result of engaging in life fully, even when it hurts

What
Happy
People
Know

CHAPTER ONE

The Dance of Love and Fear

This poor rich man—he looked so pale and drained. He was living a life that held no happiness, and he needed my help.

He had everything the world could offer—money, freedom, friends, and family—but I could see that he did not have the one thing he needed most: simple happiness.

This man was one of the wealthiest people in the American Southwest, rich in the resources that should bring happiness. At this moment, he could have been anywhere on earth, with anyone he wanted. The world of glamour, pleasure, and power was his. And yet here he was.

On the surface, he was a poster boy for the American dream, barely old enough to be a baby boomer, gliding through the good life. To most people, even the look in his eyes probably bespoke nothing darker than worldliness or weariness. However, I have spent all of my career and most of my life looking beneath the surface of human behavior, and what I saw in his eyes was haunting and familiar. I've seen that look too many times.

Fortunately, I have learned how to help people overcome what's behind that dark and empty expression. I have learned how to help them find happiness—to alchemize it out of fear, depression, boredom, and even grief. More commonly, I have helped people to locate the elusive quality of happiness in lives that should *already* have been good.

Your life probably looks pretty good to most people. These days, that's true for many of us. We've all worked so hard and attained so much. But do you often feel as if you've lost something?

That was certainly true of this man. Because he was enrolled in the 7-Day Life Enhancement Program that I direct at Canyon Ranch—one of the country's most prominent health facilities—I wouldn't have much time to spend with him. It doesn't take much time, though, to teach people how to be happy—to teach them the things that happy people already know.

And it won't take you long to learn what happy people know and to learn how to feel happy for the rest of the day. It will take longer, however, for you to work these lessons into the heart of your life, until happiness becomes a habit and unhappiness feels foreign.

This might be difficult for you, but what task could be more vital?

If you don't think happiness is critically important, perhaps it's because you have a narrow definition of it, as many people do, thinking that it just means being in a good mood most of the time, or experiencing the emotion of joy. But happiness is neither a mood nor an emotion. Mood is a biochemical condition, and emotions are just transitory feelings. Happiness is a way of life—an overriding outlook composed of qualities such as optimism, courage, love, and fulfillment. It's not just tiptoeing through the tulips of la-la land, and it's not something that changes every time your situation changes. It is nothing less than cherishing every day.

The wealthy man who had come to see me had lost his love for life. If you haven't met many wealthy people, you might think he was an aberration. You might think, "Give me that money, and I'll show you how to be happy!" The fact is that wealthy people—despite Madison Avenue's fairy tales about them—are unhappy just as commonly as people without much money. That's one important thing that happy people know: Money doesn't bring happiness.

You've heard that before, right? So you're probably thinking, "Yeah, that must be true" (and are secretly thinking, "But it doesn't apply to *me*!").

It does apply to you, though, as the new, emerging science of happiness proves. The myth that money brings happiness is one of the happiness traps that I will tell you about in this book, along with the happiness tools that will free you from these traps. Learning about these traps and tools will change your life.

If, on the other hand, you go on believing the conventional wisdom about happiness, you might never be any more fulfilled than you are at this moment, no matter how good your life gets. The traps can hold you down forever.

If you are stuck in one or more of the happiness traps, at least you're not alone. Happiness, as I'll show with research and with my own extensive clinical findings, is a relatively rare quality. Most people think that happiness is common among others—especially those with happy-face veneers—and that it is imminently available for themselves, just over the horizon, tomorrow's payoff for today's pain. In reality, happiness is not at all common in modern American society, and is even scarcer now than it was in earlier, less affluent times. In terms of happiness, America is going downhill, and has been for more than 20 years, even as our affluence has blossomed. Such a sad paradox: The more we've attained, the emptier we've become.

The man who had come to see me—let's call him Christopher Conner—was extraordinary in his affluence, exceptionally strong-willed, and charismatic in manner, but he had a lot in common with the average person.

What he mostly had in common—what we *all* have in common—is that we are brothers and sisters of the same imperfect evolution, the same flawed flesh. We all have a neurological fear system embedded deep within our brains, a neural network that once helped us survive as a species, but now limits our lives. *This biological circuitry of fear is the greatest enemy of happiness.*

This fear system is our repository for past trauma, current tribulation, fear of the future, and archaic instinctual terrors.

The forces of evolution, by their very nature, endowed this fear system with tremendous power, because in the brutal early epochs of mankind, it alone kept us alive. It gained us the hair-trigger capacity to spring into action at the first hint of threat. The automatic fear response became faster than the process of rational thought, faster than experiencing the feeling of love, faster than any other human action. And thus we survived. But in doing so, we became hardwired for hard times.

This is our legacy, like it or not.

Unfortunately, in modern life, what is good for survival is often bad for happiness and even for long-term health. What once saved us now slowly kills us.

Of course, it would be foolish to fault nature for placing survival first, because the obvious alternative is extinction. But where do we go from here? To lives of meaning and joy? Or do we settle for mere biological survival?

For most of us in modern society, survival has become a gentle affair: Go to work, pay the bills, day is done. We no longer need a pool of primal fear to propel us away from a mastodon via a fast blast of adrenaline, or to keep us awake in the dark of night, listening for threatening sounds. However, even though we usually no longer need the neurological wiring that led us out of the Stone Age, we still have it. (Evolution is excruciatingly slow: Consider the fact that humans still have tailbones.)

Luckily, we have been blessed with an almost magical source of compensation: the human neocortex. The neocortex is the primary area of intellect in the brain, located in the cerebrum. It is creative, intuitive, intellectual, and spiritual. And it is the physical site of happiness.

With our wonderfully redemptive neocortical abilities, we can override the limitations of evolution and free ourselves from the fears that thwart happiness.

Fears will keep coming up—always, always. But we can rise above them. This is our evolutionary gift—our way out of the darkness of the past, into light.

"My head's murdering me," Mr. Conner moaned as he slumped into a seat. "The market's really tanking today."

He probably expected me to sympathize, or, in the vernacular of my profession, to validate his feelings. I don't believe in the wholesale validation of feelings. Feelings can be just as screwed up as behavior. I knew that no matter what happened in the market on this day or any other, Christopher Conner would have more than enough to live a lavish lifestyle until the day he died. Nothing was murdering him on this beautiful morning—except for the fears that he was inflicting upon himself.

He'd seen several other psychologists, but they'd done little more than catalogue his feelings and corroborate his misery. This uncritical validation of feelings—which leads to the glorification of the victim role—is one of the many mistakes commonly perpetrated in the field of clinical psychology.

Clinical psychology—the treatment in a clinical setting of people with mental disorders—was begun with great fanfare as an adjunct to modern medicine in the late 1800s. It was patterned after the conventional medical model of fighting pathology. Clinical psychology was based on the assumption that most people are mentally healthy—and happy—but some people contract mental pathologies that conform to neat diagnostic compartments, and require standardized treatments. This approach sounds scientific and is generally quite lucrative.

The only problem is that it doesn't work very well. It fails approximately two-thirds of the time. Yet, despite the frequent failure of the anti-pathology approach, this system is endorsed by many of its practitioners—quite cynically, I believe—as psychology's only valid avenue.

One of the greatest deficiencies of this "cynical psychology" approach is that it was not designed to help people find happiness. It assumed that if mental illness were cured, happiness would naturally follow, as the normal human condition. But this just doesn't happen for the vast majority of people. Their fear systems get in the way.

Furthermore, I believe that even when people do not have diagnosable psychological illnesses, they still cannot be considered psychologically healthy unless they are happy. The absence of disease is not the same as health, just as the absence of poverty is not the same as wealth.

My perspective on psychology is similar to the views of physicians who practice integrative medicine. These doctors try to help their patients move beyond the mere absence of disease to the realm of robust health, in which they feel energetic, vital, and strong. In the same vein, I try to help people move beyond the mere absence of psychological disturbance to the realm of happiness, in which they feel optimistic, loving, and spiritually connected.

I believe that the quest to achieve happiness will characterize the psychology of the 21st century. It is the kind of endeavor that can change a whole culture.

I have seen this quest's power. I have seen it change lives. I thought it could change the life of Mr. Conner. And I think it can change yours.

The Failure of Success

Christopher Conner wanted to start our session by telling me about his parents. He thought it was important. His mother, he said, had grown up on a subsistence-level farm during the Depression, drinking well water from a bucket, using an outhouse, and eating only what she and her family could grow. His thick-skinned dad had survived the tenements of Brooklyn, fought in trenches against the Nazis, and worked in a noisy and dirty factory for 40 years. Their lives had apparently been hard and dark. They'd sacrificed terribly to send him to college—and had never let him forget it. As an adult, he'd suffered himself, fighting his own business-world "trench warfare" and constantly postponing his own pleasure. He'd pushed himself so hard that he'd spent his health to gain his wealth, and now his heart was a ticking time bomb. And yet, after all this, he still felt empty. Recently he'd given his son a Corvette for graduation—a 'Vette!—"And my son says, 'Dad, what I *really* wanted was a Ferrari.' And my wife backs him up! True story!" He made a face, and it was a little scary—hard-edged and angular—the expression of someone accustomed to getting his way. "Some of my friends with money, we call our kids the Royal Order of the Lucky Sperm Club. They were born on third base and think they hit a triple. Could you be happy if . . ." I gently cut him off. I didn't want to talk about the privation of his parents or the failings of his family. I wanted to talk about *him*.

I told him that I didn't think it was his work, or his upbringing, or any of his day-to-day problems that were making him miserable. I told him about the deep neurological network of fear that we all have locked inside. I said that even if he made a billion dollars this year and reconciled all his feelings about his parents, his wife, and his kids, he'd still feel about the same, and always would—until he tackled the errant and archaic hardwiring of his own brain. He needed to learn, as do we all, how to help his neocortical brain functions—his higher thought and spirit—dominate the lower brain functions that are focused solely upon survival.

At first, he denied that he was fearful. I expected that, especially from a hard charger like him. We're taught that fear is for little girls and losers. After he thought about it, though, he admitted, "I do tend to worry a lot." Then he quickly added, "But it's that worry that keeps me on top."

I've heard that claim a thousand times, but I've never swallowed it. Most successful people don't get ahead because of worry. They do it with brains and vision.

Even so, it's hard to talk anxiety lovers out of the glory of suffering. To them, it's the Red Badge of Worry. They even worry about not worrying.

"What's your biggest concern?" I asked Mr. Conner.

"Keeping what I've got. The only thing harder than making money is hanging on to it."

"I've heard other people say that." Countless times. I still don't believe it. It's just another way for successful people to justify their ongoing fear—the anxiety that money was supposed to kill.

No matter how much money people have, almost all of us want just a *little bit more*. But it never makes us happier. This is the failure of success.

"Do you get angry very often?" I asked.

"You can't run a conglomerate without kicking butts," he said with the same flashy, confident smile that I'd once seen when he was on the cover of *Forbes* magazine. "You can't even run a family." Just the way he said it sold it—what a strong personality! I could see how he'd cobbled a string of troubled TV and phone companies into a powerful communications conglomerate.

"You a perfectionist?"

"Try to be."

"Optimist or pessimist?"

"If you prepare for the worst, it doesn't happen."

"Much anxiety?"

"That comes with the territory."

"I'm guessing you feel fairly isolated."

"It's lonely at the top." Again, that million dollar smile. But I was beginning to think there was nothing behind it but fear.

"I'm also guessing you tend to get depressed."

"Lately I do."

Mr. Conner wasn't aware of it, but he was describing the many faces of fear. More often than not, fear doesn't emerge as nail-biting, cold-feet terror, but surfaces instead as anger, perfectionism, pessimism, low-level anxiety, depression, and feelings of isolation. In these many disguises, fear can permeate life, leaving room for little else. It morphs from one pseudoemotion to another, rarely declaring itself, poisoning each moment it touches.

"Other than work," I asked Mr. Conner, "how's the rest of your life?"

He gave me a blank look. "Fine." Then he described a home life that would horrify most people: alienated kids, a wife who bitterly resented his obsession with work, and never any time for just kicking back and feeling good. Work was everything, and everything else was nothing. I call this *unidimensional living*, and it's a killer.

I asked him if he ever thought about turning over more work to his associates.

"I can't," he brooded. "A lot of the decisions I make are life-or-death. Not the kinds of things I can delegate."

When he said "life-or-death," something in me clicked.

"I have a prescription for you," I said. "I want you to volunteer tomorrow at a pediatric cancer ward. I'll set it up."

"Like hell you will."

"Do you want to feel better?"

"I don't feel *that* bad."

"Why should you feel bad at *all?*"

He sat silently, unsettled—a strong man afraid to find a new kind of strength. I could almost hear him thinking, "Damn! I thought this guy's cure for stress would be more *golf!*"

The Lesser Life

Millions of Americans have become so used to not being happy that they barely even notice it. For them, it's like living next to a railroad track— after a while, you don't even hear the trains.

Even so, no matter how numb you may become, life goes on. Days become years, until life is still there but the living is gone.

Here is the kind of day—the kind of life—that countless people over the past 30 years have described to me.

> "I only wake up when I have to. There's never enough time to sleep. The kids try to be good in the morning, but they're always needing something or squabbling. Then there's traffic, watching out for the road rage weirdos, hoping I won't be late for work. Lots of the time I am, and then the boss gives me a dirty look, which puts a hollow feeling in the pit of my stomach. That's okay, because I need to be a little keyed up to stay on top of things.
>
> "I usually feel like filling that hollow feeling with a snack— something bad, like a cream cheese Danish—though I try to control my weakness for sweets because I'm too fat. The young people in the office all look so thin, and I guess I don't want to admit I'm getting older. Old isn't good at work. So I really push myself, and

sometimes my boss gives me a pat on the back, and that makes me feel good for about an hour. Then things get crazy again—or bor-r-ring—and the good feeling wears off, just like my boss's good mood. At lunch, I check the stock market, and if it's down I feel like I'm never going to be able to retire, and if it's up I start thinking about buying something. But if I do that, I'll go broke. You can't win the money game. You either do without or get sick to your stomach every time the Visa bill arrives.

"After lunch, I try to knuckle down, but just end up with a headache, thinking, will the weekend ever get here? And when it does, what'll I do—housework? It feels like I work 24/7, which is probably going to earn me nothing more than a heart attack, like my dad. He died early, which is an issue I'm still trying to resolve. A lot of people in my family have died early—heart disease, mostly—and that's why I worry about my health. I'm not complaining, though—I make twice what my dad did. God knows, I live the good life. And if I keep this up, I'm going to move up the ladder and get more control, and stop having to take orders from idiots.

"After work, I think about getting some exercise, though I usually end up going home and having a drink instead, and wishing I could have about three more—but then I'd have to put up with the snide comments. I get about as much appreciation at home as I do at work. But usually there's something good on TV, and at least I can say, 'Well, I got a lot done today.' And if somebody cares enough to ask how my day went, I can say, 'Not bad, how was yours?' And they'll say, 'Oh, it was okay.' An hour or so before I go to bed, the kids are asleep, and that's my special time, although I usually can't *keep my eyes open. I fall into a coma for about 3 hours. Then, in the middle of the night, I start getting restless. I don't sleep as well as I used to. Which is the main reason I wake up tired and want to sleep in. Obviously, though, I can't. I don't have that option."*

If that sounds a little too much like your life, don't be disturbed. It is the general lifestyle and emotional outlook described by approximately two-thirds of average American subjects in a recent study, most of whom also described themselves as "not very happy." This type of lifestyle persists even among the wealthy (although they worry about money even *more*).

This is not a life of misery, and it's certainly not one of madness. But it's not a happy life. It's a lesser life.

When you were young, you might have seen your parents living like this, and said to yourself, "That's my family, but it's not me!"

You were right. It shouldn't be you. You can do better. Much better.

The Better Life

"How was the cancer ward?"

"My God!" said Chris Conner, by way of an answer.

His eyes seemed wider, more open, as if he were still seeing something he couldn't believe he'd seen. He also looked somehow more human. He was smiling with his eyes, and not just his mouth—an accurate indicator, according to happiness researchers, of genuine joy. His limbs were looser and his expressions were softer. It's amazing how quickly people can begin to change, once they start dealing with their whole lives, and not just their feelings.

"You know," he said, "we could have sat here for hours talking about life and death, and I still wouldn't have gotten it. But when I saw those kids with tubes coming out of every part of their bodies, and the doctors hunched over their computers looking for a way to get an edge on the disease, and parents squeezing each other's hands and trying to be brave, I got it right away."

"Good! Got what?"

"That my business isn't life or death. My business is actually pretty fun. Compared."

He looked like a man who'd been freed from jail. Nothing in his life had changed—except him. But that was everything.

"Up until about noon," he said, "I thought I was handling it okay, not letting it get to me. But then I was walking down a corridor with a doctor, telling him what was wrong with his portfolio, probably making too much noise, and we pass by a room where there's a mom and dad bawling their heads off and holding each other, and I look in—because you can't help it—and just as I look in they're pulling this sheet. . . ." He stopped and pushed his lips together hard. "The nurse is pulling this sheet over a little bald-headed girl lying in bed. Not much younger than my daughter." He stopped again. "Not much younger than my Hailey— who's been at *camp* all summer." He had to stop.

"What did the little girl say to you?" Sometimes I ask unusual questions, to penetrate peoples' armor.

"Say to me?"

"Metaphorically."

"She said, 'Don't blow it with Hailey.' "

He shook his head in wonder, as if this horror had been the luckiest experience of his life. We think it's the happy experiences in life that make us happy. But it's not. "The thing is," he said, "I always thought death made life meaningless—like, what's the point? How can you be happy when you know you'll die? One day on that ward, though, and I realized death is what makes life precious. Strange! But *me*—I act like nothing matters but money." Then he gave me a look I hadn't yet seen from him: undisguised fear. He was just beginning to get it. "Why do you think I worry so much about getting richer?"

"I don't. I think you worry about being poor."

That was irrational, of course, considering his vast assets, but irrationality is what fear is all about. It hijacks the rational mind and re-creates life in its own twisted image.

"By God," he said, bumping his fist onto his knee, "I think maybe you've got a point! Every time I get worked up about some deal falling through, I get this mental picture of me working in my dad's old factory."

"Movie stars come in here—big stars—and they say, 'I'll never work in this town again!'"

"But it makes no sense."

"Fear is the opposite of sense."

Just then his cell phone bleated out the first bar of Wagner's "Ride of the Valkyries," and he grabbed it. Guys like him hate to be out of touch.

A text message began to scroll across the face of his phone. "Oh, for God's sake!" he said. It kept coming. "This is insane!" It scrolled for another half-minute.

He looked up at me, his face flushed and full of pressure from his hard-beating heart. "I just got a Dear John text message from my wife!"

His eyes went hard again. "I'm not ready for this."

He was right. He wasn't.

Like so many people, not all of them rich, Chris Conner wasn't ready to face problems that couldn't be fixed by money. He didn't have the qualities it takes—not at this point.

So what could I do for him?

Many conventional psychologists, I'm sure, would have rushed Chris and his wife into intensive, confrontive couples therapy, aimed at attacking the sublimation, repression, alienation, and other psychological maladies that seemed to be ruining their relationship. But not me. I abandoned the antiproblem approach a long time ago, for a simple reason: It didn't work. Instead, I began to look for positive possibilities, and I've gotten great results ever since.

As far as I was concerned, Christopher Conner could talk himself blue in the face about all of his problems, and still end up with nothing more than insight into his misery. Putting something under a microscope doesn't change what it is. I wanted to keep talking to Chris about some of the things we'd started to discuss before his wife's message—things like optimism, love, and courage. These were the only things that would pull him through this crisis—regardless of what his wife decided to do—because these are the qualities that propel us past pain. More important, they are the qualities that make our lives happy.

Chris didn't have enough of these qualities, and it had rendered him a leaf in the wind, vulnerable to the vagaries of fate. If his wife hadn't decided to leave him, sooner or later some other disaster would have hit.

Besides, he'd been unhappy *before* her message.

Chris told me fervently that *now* he'd be happy, if only she'd decide to stay. But I said he had it backward: If he first became happy, *then* she'd stay.

Okay then, he said, in so many words, go ahead and make me happy. He saw happiness as a finite, discrete entity unto itself, like the Hope Diamond or the Mona Lisa—something he could get drop-shipped from Paris or Caracas.

But happiness never comes all at once. Happiness, in the final analysis, is a catchall term for the condition that comes from several indispensable qualities. It's a by-product.

The sum of the following qualities is happiness. Not all of these qualities must be present for happiness to exist, and they don't all have to be there in equal amounts. Most of them must be abundant, though, for someone to experience the kind of lasting, rock-solid happiness that endures even when life gets tough to take—as it always does, sooner or later.

The 12 Qualities of Happiness

1. **Love.** This is the wellspring of happiness, renewable and everlasting. We often think that being loved is the best feeling in the world, but it's the second best. The best is loving someone else. Love is the polar opposite of fear, emotionally and neurologically. Thus, it is the antidote to fear and the first step toward happiness.

2. **Optimism.** Optimism provides power over painful events. I used to think it was an attitude: seeing a glass as half-full instead of half-empty. But that felt artificial, a mere trick of perception. Then I suffered the worst event of my life. My son died. I thought the light had left my life forever. However, in my despair, I realized that my son had left me a legacy of love that was mine forever, and that if I could survive the loss of my child, nothing else could devastate me. When I realized this, I found that every hurtful event holds lessons, and that the more it hurts, the more you learn. Thus, I discovered the

true meaning of optimism. Optimism is realizing that the more painful the event, the more profound the lesson. Once you bring this knowledge into your heart, you can never again look at any event as all bad. Optimism gives you power over fear of the future and over regret for the past.

3. **Courage.** This is your strongest weapon for overcoming the split-second power of the fear system. You can't rise above fear without courage, because fear is hardwired into your neural circuitry. There is no such thing as a "fear-ectomy." If fear is eternally programmed into your brain, though, so is courage. It comes from the neocortex and is a product of the spirit, the intellect, and the higher emotions of love and generosity. It is nature's natural balance for the fear that has helped us survive. It's the quality that allows us to thrive.

4. **A sense of freedom.** Nothing fills the soul like freedom. Freedom is choice, and choice is what makes us human. When we choose, we define who we are. Everyone has the power to make choices, but unhappy people don't know they have it. They think it's only for the rich. It's not. I've met a thousand rich people who didn't feel free. Choice is available to anyone who has the courage to exercise it.

5. **Proactivity.** Happy people participate in their own destinies and forge their own happiness. They don't wait for events or other people to make them happy. They're not passive victims.

6. **Security.** Happy people know that nothing, over time, lasts—not money, not approval, not even life itself. So they don't measure security with a calendar or a calculator. They simply like who they are. They're not slaves to popularity, longevity, or financial status. They know that security is an inside job.

7. **Health.** Happiness and health are interdependent. It's hard to be happy if you don't feel healthy, and it's hard to be healthy if you're not happy. Of special importance for happiness is healthy mood chemistry. You can have a happy life and not even know it if you're tortured by faulty mood chemistry. An imbalance of the neurotransmitters serotonin and dopamine, for example, can mask the happiness that lies beneath it.

8. **Spirituality.** Happy people aren't afraid to go beyond the boundaries of their own lives. They let go, and welcome extraordinary experiences. They have markedly less fear of death. They're not concerned about dying—they're concerned about not living.

9. **Altruism.** Unhappy people are usually too self-absorbed to be altruistic. But happy people know how good it feels. It connects you to others, gives you a purpose, and gets you outside yourself.

10. **Perspective.** Unhappy people tend to see things in absolute terms and often can't distinguish small problems from big ones. Happy people see shades of gray, and they know how to prioritize their problems and turn them into possibilities. They don't lose sight of life's big picture during bad times.

11. **Humor.** Humor is a shift of perception that gives people the guts to go on when life looks its worst. There is an abandonment in it that is close to enlightenment. It lifts suffering off the heart and hands it to the intellect and spirit, which alone have the power to heal it.

12. **Purpose.** Happy people know why they're here on earth. They're doing the things they were meant to do. If they died today, they would be satisfied with their lives.

These are the qualities that collectively compose happiness, and the qualities that I most often talk about with the guests at Canyon Ranch. If they achieve these qualities, they no longer need to search for happiness—it finds them.

Of course, a few other important qualities count, too, such as self-esteem, peace of mind, fulfillment, and confidence. But the list isn't as long as you might think. Happiness is profound, but simple.

People often presume that these are qualities you're born with. Not always. But you can acquire them—by mastering the use of the happiness tools and avoiding the fear-inspired happiness traps. When people acquire these qualities, it gives them a lift like no other. They get out of bed in the morning after a peaceful sleep, eager to tackle their challenges. They can't wait to share the experiences of their daily lives with their families, coworkers, and friends. They don't hop from one worry to the next, fixating on their bank accounts, their bosses, their waistlines, or their status.

With this new outlook, people invariably fall in love with life, and often begin to feel, they tell me, "like a kid again." That's natural. In childhood, our spirits were unbridled and unbroken. We still had our neurological network of fear—our bogeymen under the bed—but our spirits led the way.

As we get older, though, and have to solve all our own problems, we become increasingly obsessed with what it takes to survive in this world. Our basic balance begins to shift—from spirit to survival—and we lose our love for life. Ultimately, we find that the things we have to do to survive are often the things that end up killing us.

But if we find a way to keep the qualities of happiness, the spirit stays strong. Life can still hurt us, but it cannot destroy what is in us.

One day, of course, we will die—but not without first having lived.

And as we live, we will still shed tears—but will always return to a place of peace.

This is the grace that these qualities grant. This grace creates the power—the inner authority—that Christopher Conner, despite his formidable strength, still did not have.

The Power of Appreciation

Chris Conner looked like death warmed over. The pallor that had chalked his face on his first visit was becoming a necrotic gray. For years, he'd skated by on his willpower and toughness, but that wasn't getting him through this. I made a mental note to schedule him with our cardiologist.

"How are you feeling?" I asked.

He mulled it over, as if searching for what hurt worst in a world of hurt. "Humiliated," he said finally.

"There's something good you can get from that."

"Let's talk about my marriage."

"I am."

"Okay," he said, as if humoring me, "what good can I get from humiliation?"

"Humility. You ever watch those awards shows on TV, where the winner says, 'I feel so humbled by this honor?' Well, it's not honor that teaches humility. It's humiliation."

"Lucky me."

"Hey, you paid the tuition—you might as well learn the lesson. And be realistic: For you, humility is worth its weight in gold. You've got a strong ego—that's your gift—but it's gotten you into trouble, especially at home. Tell me this. What makes the humiliation hurt so much?"

He answered quietly. All the bluster and bravado had been knocked out of him. "Thinking maybe I'm not good enough for her."

To my way of thinking, that was a survival fear. Contemporary fear, I've found, almost always fits into one of two categories: *fear of not having enough* and *fear of not being enough*. Having enough and being enough are the two factors that best ensure survival, so fears about them are rooted to the core of the neurological fear system. They're as deep as the fear of death, and they are closely related to it.

For years, Chris Conner had fixated on not having enough, and now he was dangerously close to obsessing about not being enough. I had to head him off. Once a fear like that takes hold, it's hard to stop.

He would always be vulnerable to these two fears: We all are. But he had powers—as do we all—that he could use to rise above them. And he was almost ready—almost opened enough by pain—to hear what they were.

"Have you talked to your wife?" I asked.

"She finally returned one of my calls."

"What did you talk about?"

"Mostly? Believe it or not, this girl at 7-Eleven."

I gave him a quizzical look.

"Just before Sarah called, I was driving around, thinking, Should I call my lawyers, or what? And I stopped at a 7-Eleven for a Coke—you know, no booze at the Ranch—and I'm standing there, feeling crappy, and this girl behind the counter is taking her sweet time, like my time's worth bupkes. I was pissed. Lotta nerve! And right in the middle of this

Sarah calls, and I tell her to hang on, because this girl's jerking me around, and Sarah sticks up for the *girl*—which doesn't improve my mood—and I tell Sarah about seeing the little girl in the hospital die and how it really changed me. And she says, 'It doesn't *sound* like you've changed,' and that was about the end of it. Long story short, she hasn't moved out. Yet."

It was time. Now or never.

"Tell me what you appreciate about Sarah."

He looked disoriented. Good. I was taking him down a whole new path.

He started out mentioning mundane things—pretty face, good education—and slowly picked up steam. "I guess I mostly love her kindness—to me, the kids, everybody. And she's not selfish like I am. She has friends, not just business friends. She . . ." He went on and on, and an extraordinary change came over him. He began to seem more like he had when he'd just come back from the cancer ward: gentler, deeper.

"What do you appreciate about your son?"

"He's a tiger," Chris said with his big, flashy smile. "You should see him on a tennis court."

"And your daughter?"

"Hailey," he said in a sugary voice, "little Hailey—she has the most beautiful hair. It's like the sun."

"Are you maybe thinking about the little girl who died? Who lost her hair?"

"I guess I am. I can't shake it."

"Chris, the love we have in our lives, we can lose it. Just as we eventually lose our lives. Love is not a given."

"I'm starting to realize that. It's scary."

"But it's like you said, the specter of loss is what makes life precious. Love, too."

For a moment, he seemed to sense the beauty in this brutal paradox, but then his eyes grew tight again. Happiness isn't easy. It takes time.

"Right now," he said, "I just feel scared. I can't see past my problems."

"Your problems aren't your real problem."

Your Problems Are Not Your Problem

Chris Conner's worst problem—and yours, too—is one you have always had, and always will have: Part of your brain is dedicated solely to fear. You have a biological fear system that will challenge your happiness until the day you die.

When I first started studying for my doctorate, I didn't learn much about the biology of the fear system. Most psychologists don't. We're trained to work with minds, not bodies.

But I was frustrated by this narrow view. I felt that I was missing the big picture of human behavior. In my postgraduate study, I was drawn to a relatively rare specialty called medical psychology, which acknowledges the role of biology in the mind and emotions. And I discovered—big surprise!—that people consist of minds *and* bodies.

Then, when I started working as a medical psychologist with actual human beings, I found that there was one more piece to the puzzle: the spirit. Sometimes when our minds and bodies are shattered by life, it's only the spirit that can knit us whole and keep us alive.

Your mind, body, and spirit, working in concert, can make you happy.

But this may never happen unless you first understand the single biggest enemy of your happiness: your neurological fear network. We think of fear as just a thought, but it's not. The fabric of fear has been woven into our brains, creating a neurological entity that has lasted as long as mankind.

The fear system is insidious and full of deceit. When we are tormented by the many faces of fear—perfectionism, obsession, insecurity, shyness, guilt—we often try to make sense of our pain by assuming that something is wrong with our lives: It's my wife! It's my job! It's this traffic! When we can't find anything to blame, we often make trouble, so that our outer lives will at least match our inner turmoil.

But your chronic angst will only make sense when you understand the biology of the fear system. Here it is.

The first element of the fear system is the brain stem, which is one of three basic areas of the brain and is the first part of the brain that is formed in the womb. The brain stem was also the first part of the brain to evolve in animals, 100 million years ago. Back then, the first animals to walk the earth, the reptiles, had only brain stems. Because of this, the brain stem is often referred to as the reptilian brain. I love that description, because it's a perfect metaphor for the fear that festers inside this part of the brain.

The reptilian brain holds instinctual fears and is incapable of higher thought. It cannot process complex emotions, such as love. That's why reptiles don't make good pets. A lizard will never learn its name or love its owner.

There's also another storage area for fear, which is located in the second part of the brain to evolve, the mammalian brain. The mammalian brain was first seen in evolution when mammals joined reptiles on the earth. In the womb, it's the second part of the human brain to develop. Residing in the mammalian brain is the other important culprit in the neurological symphony of fear: the amygdala. The amygdala is a memory center for emotion. In particular, it stores memories of all of your painful and threatening experiences. It's a veritable haunted house of memory. The amygdala isn't as primordial as the brain stem; it does have some power to evaluate fears—though not much. It's a primitive warehouse for everything that's frightening.

The amygdala is directly connected to the action portion of your fear system: the endocrine glands, which produce hormones. Hormones have many functions, including protecting the body from danger and ensuring survival. The primary survival hormones are adrenaline and cortisol, which are sometimes referred to as stress hormones. They could also be called fear hormones. These hormones enable you to run faster and fight harder. They trigger the release of excitatory neurotransmitters in the brain that increase alertness. In doing so, though, they create most of the physical symptoms of fear, such as increased heart rate, high blood pressure, the sensation of butterflies in the stomach, cold feet, jitteriness, and insomnia. These physical symptoms, in turn, reinforce the emotional feeling of fear and can create a spiral of anxiety.

When the human brain stem, amygdala, and endocrine system evolved more than a million years ago, they were incredibly helpful, because back then virtually all threats to survival were physical. In early times, people literally ran off their extra stress hormones. In our modern world, though, this fear system is often harmful, because the threats we face today are generally abstract: higher interest rates, disapproval from the boss, or too many bills. When you're sitting at a desk, it's not helpful to have your heart pounding and your blood pressure rocketing. In fact, it can be deadly.

Even so, we're stuck with the biological remnants of the past. For as long as we live, each of us must listen to this symphony of fear, conducted by the reptilian brain and amygdala.

Fortunately, though, the fear system can be overruled by the third major part of the brain, the neocortex. The neocortex was the last part of the brain created during evolution, and it is the last part of the brain that is developed in the womb.

The human neocortex is the crowning achievement of evolution. It's the site of the intellect, which performs incredible cognitive feats, such as abstract reasoning and the storage of long-term memories. The neocortex is also the physical site of the human spirit, the entity that links the intellect with intuition and the subconscious. The human spirit goes beyond the boundaries of reason and experience, and can often seem to know the unknowable.

The neocortex evaluates the messages from the two lower areas of the brain, including the constant cries of fear that bubble up from the reptilian brain and amygdala. It has the amazing ability to say, "Nothing is wrong—calm down!"

Sometimes these messages of reassurance come directly from the intellect, and other times they come more from the spirit, with its mint of intuitive knowledge.

These messages are our saving grace. Bursting forth from the neocortex, our crown of evolution, these messages of comfort and confidence are our ultimate reward for having evolved.

However, we often fail to hear them, and remain deafened by the white noise of fear. Why do we let this happen? Because sometimes it's easier. Because fear comes fast. Because we get overwhelmed or exhausted. Because that's what our parents did. Because therapists validate our feelings.

Because we're human.

In every one of us, there is a delicate and shifting balance between the power of the reptilian brain and the power of the neocortex. I call this oscillating balance the dance of the spirit and the reptile.

The spirit must lead. That is the key to happiness.

Change

Chris was back, and his color was better. He'd been getting some sun and exercise, and it had put some pink where there had been only pallor. He may also have been responding to a mild antidepressant, though it was probably too early for it to kick in. He was only taking a small dose, but it was enough to give him a serotonin hedge against his adrenal edge. In addition, he appeared to be benefiting from some mood stabilizing supplements.

Already, his cardiovascular indices were improving. His mind, body, and spirit seemed to be gaining strength, despite his marital crisis—or maybe because of it.

"Toughest week of my life!" he said, as he settled into a chair. But he acted as if he were energized. "I just talked to Sarah."

"How'd it go?"

"It went well." He seemed surprised. "For once, I let her do the talking. I mostly just talked about that little girl I saw die—I can't get her out of my mind—and the girl at the convenience store."

"The 7-Eleven clerk?"

"Yeah, I saw her again, and the damnedest thing happened. I was buying some bottled water, and there she is, on the phone again, but for whatever reason, it's not getting to me. Maybe because of some of the things we've been talking about, like my worry and how it makes me feel rushed. Next thing I know, she's standing at the register but she can hardly function, she's so bummed out. Tears in her eyes, the works. So I say, 'Tough day?' and she just nods. But I draw her out, and after a while I'm getting the story of her life. Problem is, her mom's dying of cancer and wants to try a different approach—a chemo thing in Houston—and the insurance company should cover it, but they're dragging their feet. Red tape. Forms. Stuff getting lost. The usual. Meanwhile, the poor mom—my God! You don't want to hear the details. Well, it turns out that the insurance company is a subsidiary of a company I've partnered with. I know the CEO well. So I give her my card and write the name of one of my VPs on it, so she can call and say she's a friend and get him to light a fire under the insurance company."

His face was beginning to glow with happiness. Not from any anti-depressant, or supplement, or runner's high. It was coming from the in-side out, as true happiness always does.

"Well, you'd think I'd given her the Taj Mahal! She leans over the counter and gives me . . ." He stopped abruptly and swallowed hard. In a shaky voice he said, ". . . this big hug. And she says . . ." He had to stop again. "'You're a good man.'" His eyes were shiny, but he fired up a grin—one from the heart—that lit the room.

At this moment in his life, Christopher Conner was ready—more than ready—to hear, in plain and simple terms, everything I have ever learned about happiness. A magazine article had once called Chris "a survivor," marveling at his toughness and street smarts, but now he was becoming much more than that. Like many exceptionally strong people, his will was enabling him to no longer just survive, but to begin also to thrive. The same energy can go to either ambition, and Chris had finally found that thriving is a much higher calling than mere surviving.

I started talking, and Chris, bless him, started taking notes. I don't know how long I talked, maybe an hour or two. At the end of it, he had about 20 pages of notes, and I asked if I could photocopy them.

Those notes were the inspiration for this book. When I looked back at them in black and white, I realized that they were something I should share with as many people as possible.

The information in the notes was an amalgam of good science, good sense, and a lifetime of learning the things that happy people know.

They boiled down to just six basic psychological mechanisms for achieving happiness—which I now call happiness tools—and five negative forces, or traps.

In the next chapter, I'll alert you to the traps and tell you of the tools that can set you free. As the book unfolds, you'll see that avoiding the traps and using the tools is a tremendous challenge. Being miserable is easy. Being happy is hard.

Being happy means turning a deaf ear to fear, even when it's screaming for attention. It means being your true self, even when it hurts. It means going after what you really want, even when you don't think you'll get it.

It means letting your spirit lead in the dance of the spirit and the reptile.

Are you ready?

The End of the Beginning

"You look relaxed," I told Chris as he walked in.

"I should. This is my last day here."

"Sorry to go?"

He nodded. "But I miss my family. More than I ever did on any business trip."

"So, is Sarah staying?"

"I'm not certain yet. She talked about needing more time alone. Whatever that means. She's going to call."

"You scared?"

"Not like before. I'll be okay, either way. Whatever happens, I'm going to live a little. You know, I can't make her love me. All I can do is love her."

"Is that enough?"

"It's all there is."

He was right. That's all there is.

His cell phone rang. He checked the caller ID.

"It's her."

"I'll leave you alone."

He motioned for me to stay.

I could hear his end of the call. "Hi . . . I'm with Dan . . . Mostly just thinking . . . About what it must have been like to be married to me all these years . . . I think I understand—now . . . Of course I'll promise that. . . ." He began to smile. His wife talked for some time. "Give her a kiss for me. I'll see you soon. Bye."

It was a simple call between two people who had already said all the words there are to say.

His eyes, distant during the call, came back, and for the first time I saw peace in them.

"She said all she wants is to not be the last person on my callback sheet."

"That doesn't sound so hard."

"You've never seen my callback sheet." He started to laugh. The million dollar smile! But with it now were tears, too, the nourishing force of his newborn happiness. He blinked them back—not in repression, but in the simple determination to stay a strong man, as always—with strength itself as his greatest asset.

His life, thank God, would never be the same.

CHAPTER TWO

The Money Trap

So Chris and Sarah lived happily ever after, right? Isn't that the way these psychology books are supposed to go? Guy has a problem, meets the Great Doctor, gets cured, lives happily ever after?

Well . . . for starters, forget the "ever" part. Nobody's happy forever—not in the real world. That's something happy people know.

Who'd even want to be happy all day long, every day of his life? If someone told you that you could somehow never again be hungry, would you go for it? Never be thirsty? Never have yearnings yet to be met?

If that happened, how would you even know what satisfaction felt like?

There can be no wave without a trough—nor happiness, either, without some sadness to set it off.

What was Chris's problem? It was the same one he'd come in with, of course—garden-variety greed. All his life, he'd used money to fight his fear, and you don't escape that kind of pattern overnight. Especially when money is concerned: Money can have almost demonic power.

I've seen guests change at the Ranch, and go home and change right back. But then they return, and the next time it lasts—until the market crashes, or their husband dies, or they make a billion bucks, and are blasted into a whole new world. People do change—but things change, too, and it can be hard to keep up.

Even so, there's such a thing as a pivotal point in the lives of most people, and Christopher Conner had reached his. He was not the same man.

When he first went home, he spent an idyllic year focusing on his family. But that took a toll at work, problems mounted, and after a while he increasingly began to settle for the automatic fear response, which just made things worse. His relationship with Sarah suffered.

But wisdom, once earned, cannot be forgotten or easily unlearned. Chris had finally recognized what his money could do—and what it couldn't. So when his reptile reared its head—screaming, "I need more, more, more!"—he gradually realized that he would always be vulnerable to the fear of not having enough. And with this gut-level realization came a new kind of security. Before long, he didn't even consider his occasional money fears to be a problem. They were just another opportunity to assert his strength—and win. His spirit soared.

As he found the wisdom that had always been in his heart, Chris adopted the use of the happiness tools as a way of life.

Here are the tools. Use them. They can give you, too, a second chance at life.

The Six Happiness Tools

1. **Appreciation.** This is the first and most fundamental happiness tool. Appreciation is the purest, strongest form of love. It is the outward-bound kind of love that asks for nothing and gives everything. Research now shows that it is physiologically impossible to be in a state of appreciation and a state of fear at the same time. Thus, appreciation is the antidote to fear. Although fear was the first feeling that developed during evolution, love is believed to be the second. It, too, has tremendous survival value; our early ancestors, who fought to survive during the day, huddled together for comfort at night. Fear is strong, but love is stronger, because it's a product of the neocortex, not the lower brain.

2. **Choice.** Choice is the father of freedom and the voice of the heart. Having no choices, or options, feels like being in jail. It leads to depression, anxicty, and thc condition called learned helplessness. Choice can even govern perception. Anyone can choose the course of their lives, but only happy people do it. Unhappy people make the mistake of giving in to the automatic fear reaction, which limits their choices drastically, to just fighting, fleeing, or freezing. Happy people turn away from fear, and find that their intellects and spirits contain a vast warehouse of choices.

3. **Personal power.** This is the almost indefinable proactive force, similar to character, that gives you power over your feelings and power over your fate. Personal power has two components: taking responsibility

and taking action. It means realizing that your life belongs to you and you alone, and then doing something about it. Personal power keeps you from being a victim. When your personal power is at its peak, you're secure. You don't need to be popular; you don't need to be right; you don't even need money in the bank. You can handle whatever life dishes out.

4. **Leading with your strengths.** When you give in to the automatic fear reaction, it makes you focus on your weaknesses, which only reinforces your fear. But when you take the path of the intellect and spirit, you naturally begin to focus on your strengths—and start to solve your situation. People often think that fixing their weaknesses will save them, but it rarely works. It's just too painful. Leading with your strengths feels good, and that's why it works. Simple but true. You'll never be complete until you learn to lead with your strengths every day.

5. **The power of language and stories.** We don't describe the world we see—we see the world we describe. Language, as the single most fundamental force of the human intellect, has the power to alter perception. We think in words, and these words have the power to limit us or to set us free; they can frighten us or evoke our courage. Similarly, the stories we tell ourselves about our own lives eventually become our lives. We can tell healthy stories or horror stories. The choice is ours.

6. **Multidimensional living.** There are three primary components of life: relationships, health, and purpose (which is usually work). Many people, though, put all their energy into just one area. The most common choice is work, because work best assuages our survival fears of not having enough and not being enough. Other people become obsessed with relationships (because relationship is another

word for love), and some people limit their lives in the name of longevity. None of this works. Happiness comes from a full life.

Using these tools, Chris Conner went on to live happily. But it was never easy for him. It's never easy for anybody, because happiness is surrounded by traps. And all these traps have tricks. If they couldn't trick you, they couldn't capture you.

The essential trick of the happiness traps is that they seem to offer the solution to happiness, even as they destroy any chance of ever achieving it. They seem to fight fear—but they don't: It's an illusion. One of the cruelest paradoxes of life is that the things we so often seek to soothe our souls are the very things that ultimately feed our fears and cause happiness to forever recede before us, just out of reach. And as we endlessly grasp for it we think, "It's so close!"—as life slips away and happiness fades to a dream or a memory, or, most cruel of all, begins to seem like nothing more than myth.

Over the past three decades, as I've listened to thousands of life stories about the central drama of life—the battle between fear and happiness—I've found that there are five primary traps that ensnare people who are trying with all their hearts to be happy. Chris Conner was a sucker for the money trap, but each of these traps is uniquely seductive, and each has been capturing people for thousands of years.

The Five Happiness Traps

1. **Trying to buy happiness**
2. **Trying to find happiness through pleasure**
3. **Trying to be happy by resolving the past**

4. Trying to be happy by overcoming weaknesses

5. Trying to force happiness

In all prior generations, the wisest people warned others of the various happiness traps. Many people doubtless heeded these warnings, but most probably didn't, just as most people don't these days. Those who have failed to listen, then and now, have probably felt as if this wisdom applied to others, but not them: "*You* can't find happiness through pleasure, but give me a shot at it!"

Fortunately, though, there is now a new science of happiness, and the findings of science are, for most people, more compelling than the opinions of even the wisest sages.

This new science proves, with cold facts and hard figures, that the same basic principles about happiness apply to virtually everyone, across all age groups, nationalities, and cultures. Science strips away the tricks of the happiness traps and lights the way to a more fulfilling future.

As I have worked in the development of this science, I've become increasingly fascinated by a particular question: Where did we go so wrong?

Where We Went Wrong

We went wrong, paradoxically, simply by evolving. Over the past several millennia, mankind's intellectual and spiritual development has significantly accelerated; our neocortical abilities—unparalleled in the known universe—have become far richer and more sophisticated than they were in earlier epochs. However, over the same millennia, our essential neural anatomy, first created about a million years ago, has remained relatively unchanged. So, now we're running space-age intellectual software with Stone Age neurological hardware.

This contradiction has given birth to one of the most fascinating new branches of psychology—evolutionary psychology. The basic premise of evolutionary psychology is that modern people are still strongly influenced by age-old drives, which became hardwired into the brain during hundreds of thousands of years of evolution. As E. O. Wilson, the father of evolutionary psychology, puts it, "Human nature is a hodgepodge of special genetic adaptations to an environment largely vanished, the world of the Ice Age hunter-gatherer."

One example of a modern social behavior that appears to be influenced by primitive drives has been cited by Dr. David Lykken, one of my fellow pioneers in the science of happiness. According to Dr. Lykken, a study of 50 contemporary societies indicates that when divorce occurs in a first marriage, it is by far most likely to occur during the fourth year. Four years is the length of time it takes to rear a child past the period of lactation, which was an important milestone in precivilized eras, critical to a child's survival. Thus, modern people appear to be neurologically programmed to stay in unsuccessful marriages for at least 4 years, even though the practical necessity for this behavior vanished long ago.

Archaic, fear-inspired urges also strongly influence the way we feel about the most insidious of all the happiness traps. This trap has enslaved the hearts and souls of people since the beginning of civilization.

It's money.

Happiness Trap #1: Trying to Buy Happiness

"They say that he who dies with the most toys, wins," the 48-year-old Texas oil exec said to me, as his fingers fretted with a gold button on the sleeve of his cashmere sport coat. He was trying to convince me—convince himself, really—that it was a good idea for him to take a new job. The job that was being offered to him would allow him to buy two new "toys" that he'd always wanted, a boat and a plane.

However, he already had an eight-passenger turboprop plane and a 52-foot oceangoing yacht, so I asked him if his new job involved big money.

"It does. Total compensation pencils out at one unit over a 3-year contract."

"One what?"

"Sorry. A unit is a hundred million." He paused, and scanned my face. "Dollars."

"They must really want you."

"Not as much as I want that plane."

I told him it sounded like lust to possess—desire divorced from need: what I call wanton wanting (or, translated into Texan, wanton wantin'). But he was already off and running on a long-winded description about what the plane could do: cruise at 60,000 feet, hit 600 mph, speak Japanese, make soufflés—I don't know what all. The kind of twin engine Falcon 50 he wanted hadn't even existed until the year before. "I've been hunting for a plane like this for a long time," he said, with a ravenous look in his eyes.

I still recall that he used the word "hunting," because at the time it fit perfectly with a theory I'd been developing: that material acquisitiveness stems partly from the primordial urge to hunt—an urge that enabled the early hunter-gatherers to survive. I understand that urge, because I've been a hunter myself since I was a kid. For me, there's nothing quite like the feeling of becoming totally immersed in nature, getting on an animal's wavelength, and then bringing home game to feed the family. It's as satisfying to me as other deeply primal activities, such as sitting in front of a hot, popping fire, or floating in a crystalline lagoon of warm blue water.

At Canyon Ranch, I often hear people talk about hunting—for diamonds, planes, houses, paintings, and boats—but what I really hear, beneath the surface of their conversation, is people talking about hunting down the one big prize that will finally free them from the two basic, survivalist fears that have haunted people since the Stone Age: the fears of not having enough and of not being enough.

Many of the people I counsel become fixated upon their hunts. In the heat of the hunt, they often feel a keyed-up, hyperalert sense of excitement—which they generally mistake for happiness—but once the hunt is done, they're almost never satisfied.

Their dissatisfaction, I think, stems partly from the restless, nomadic instincts of our prehistoric ancestors. In early times, when our present-day neural anatomy was still being forged, it was impossible for our ancestors ever to have enough or be enough. Survival was too uncertain. As soon as one hunt ended, the food from that hunt would begin to spoil and more would be needed. It was feast or famine. The concept of scarcity became such a constant that it was literally burned into the neuronal networks of those hardy few who did manage to have enough—the survivors, our direct forefathers.

Strange as it sounds, the executive who wanted the bigger plane was troubled by a vague, constant sense of scarcity—I need more!—which he thought his elaborate toys could ameliorate. With them, he believed, he could finally become the Alpha Male, the King of the Hill: the survivor.

It took some doing, but I eventually convinced him that simply making more money and then spending it wouldn't make him any happier. It would actually make him less happy, because he'd have to tie himself down to a job for which he had no passion. Forget the money, I said, and follow your heart.

I asked him to try to find a job he really loved. Nobody gets out of my office without vowing to actually do something. It's not enough to just talk. Talk is cheap (unless it's with a Park Avenue psychiatrist).

And—good for him!—he did do something. Something hard and real. He got a job at an animal shelter, caring for stray dogs. He washed one mangy mutt after another, fed them, got them healthy and sleek, and then used his consummate sales skills to talk people into adopting them. The first day on that job, he felt like he was going crazy. The work was dirty, humiliating, and focused on everything but him. Stripped of his status, he had to try to be happy with who he was, instead of what he was. Then, when his fortune didn't suddenly evaporate, when people still seemed to like him, and when the world didn't collapse without him helping to run it, he began to go sane. He realized that he had enough, and his job convinced him that he was enough: He was compassionate and newly humble, and he was the life-or-death difference in the lives of his beloved dogs. He later told me that it was the best job he had ever had. He eventually moved on to another job that also made him happy. He said that emotionally satisfying work was the only kind of work that he'd ever again do, and to hell with the toys. He didn't need them anymore.

He was a brave and extraordinary man. Could you walk away from that kind of money to seek your soul? But it brought him things he never would have found by just flying a faster plane: a sense of altruism, freedom, fulfillment, and peace of mind—happiness.

Most people never become this wise about money. They fall for all the tricks of the money trap. But the new science of happiness exposes these tricks.

The most important message that the science of happiness tells us about money is, almost nobody thinks they have enough. In the dark recesses of our brains, free-floating fear tells us that we need more, more, more—or our very survival will be threatened.

In an important Roper Survey, in which people were asked which of 13 basic elements of their lives they were most satisfied with, they expressed the least satisfaction with the amount of money they had.

Virtually no one feels rich. In a Gallup Poll, the respondents, on average, said that 21 percent of all Americans were rich. But only one-half of 1 percent said that they themselves were rich. People making $10,000 a year believed that those who made $50,000 were rich, and those who made $50,000 thought that people making $200,000 were rich. Those making $200,000 were still scared of their burgeoning bills and feeling the heat of perceived scarcity.

Face facts: Scarcity is burned into your brain. You'll probably never feel as if you have enough money. It's time for you to accept this. And rise above it.

Unfortunately, though, the growing trend in our society is to deny that the feeling of scarcity is an immutable constant, an ingrained fear that should be handed over to the intellect and spirit. Most people, instead, are hell-bent upon trying to soothe their feelings of scarcity by just amassing more money. For example, in a survey of college students, the percentage of those who yearned for financial success above all else almost doubled from 1970 to 1990, reaching 74 percent. Over the same period of time, the percentage of those who primarily aspired to have a meaningful life decreased from 76 percent to 43 percent.

Americans, in particular, are obsessed with money. In a recent large survey, 89 percent of the Americans who were polled said that the United States is "far too materialistic." But approximately the same percentage said that they wanted even more for themselves.

To that end, Americans are working harder than ever—almost 1 full week per year longer now than during the 1990s. Until the mid-1990s, Japanese workers averaged the longest hours of anyone in the world, but now Americans work an average of $3\frac{1}{2}$ weeks per year more than the Japanese. We also work $6\frac{1}{2}$ weeks more than the British, and 12 weeks more than German workers.

This rampant, metastasizing materialism is not making our society happier. It's making us miserable. Virtually every one of the recent studies on money and happiness indicates that money makes people significantly happier only when it relieves abject poverty. Beyond that, money just doesn't do much for happiness. It doesn't matter whether you spend your money at Tiffany or Target—no amount makes a significant difference.

When people yearn for money, though, they don't realize that they're being driven by an innate sense of scarcity. They think they're being practical. Productive. Wise. They think money will bring five important elements to their lives that will make them happy.

For Sale: Things That People Think Will Bring Happiness

1. A life of leisure
2. Status
3. Possessions
4. Financial security
5. Worldly power

These elements, people think, will make them feel as if they have enough and are good enough. This is a reasonable assumption, one that people have been making for thousands of years.

But it's just not true.

Happy people know this. And science proves it.

Does a Life of Leisure Increase Happiness?

Leisure is one of those luxuries that's best in small portions. When it's all there is to life, it's as boring as being locked in jail.

Leisure presents a terrible quandary for people with money. Either they don't have enough of it because they're always working, or they don't work at all and are drowning in it.

All of us, to some extent, create fairy tales about how good life must be for wealthy people, because we get vicarious pleasure from it, and because we think we might someday strike it rich. One of the tales we tell ourselves is that wealth and leisure are a comfortable, complementary pair. Science shows that that's usually not true.

The vast majority of millionaires in America are self-made, and one of the primary ways they gain their wealth is by sacrificing their leisure and freedom. I've met hundreds of these people, and they almost all work extremely hard—probably even harder than you do. Next time you walk through the first-class cabin on an airplane, check out how many of the passengers have their faces buried in paperwork or laptops. Is that your idea of leisure? Most of these people don't feel free; they feel frazzled.

All too often, people become financially successful by just following money—engaging in high-paying jobs they don't really like. They may look free, but they feel like prisoners. When happy people choose their jobs, they don't follow money—they follow their passions. When they do this, they tend not to worry too much about money, even if they're relatively poor, because they know they won't have to suffer to make more of it.

Ironically, people who follow their hearts often end up with plenty of money, because they usually become highly proficient at their work and they enjoy working long hours. Loving your job is the ultimate freedom. It means, in effect, that you never have to work—you just play hard and collect your check. You can't beat that for leisure.

Some people, though, are rich without having to work. They inherit money, marry someone who's rich, win the lottery, or make their fortune early in life. It looks as if they've got it made. But science clearly shows that these people have happiness levels that are only very slightly higher than average. Usually, having a lot of money and no obligations feels good for only a short time. Boredom soon sets in, along with a feeling of worthlessness and ennui. Too much leisure is oppressive, a void that's impossible to fill.

One of the most fascinating studies done on achieving wealth without work was a study of lottery winners performed by Dr. Ronnie Janoff-Bulman and her colleagues. The researchers compared 22 winners of major lotteries to 22 average people, and also to 29 victims of sudden paralysis. They found that after a temporary rush of jubilation, the lottery winners were no happier than the control group of average people and had even lost much of the joy that comes from small pleasures. They also found that once the paralysis victims got over the shock of their misfortune, they were not nearly as unhappy as might be expected. Furthermore, the paralyzed people had an even greater capacity for enjoying small pleasures than the lottery winners. Believe it or not, they were even more optimistic about future happiness than the lottery winners!

In a similar vein, other studies indicate that it's not the circumstances of our lives that determine our happiness. Two large studies showed that midlife crisis is a myth. People at midlife are every bit as happy as younger people. Another large study revealed that the so-called empty nest syndrome is also a sham—a product of the pathologizing of America by cynical psychologists. Furthermore, research shows that African Americans, though sometimes disadvantaged by discrimination, are just as happy as Caucasians. These powerful studies prove that it's neither fate nor fortune that has the most influence over our levels of happiness: It's us.

In the final analysis, leisure is a state of mind. When most people talk about leisure, they're really talking about the relaxation and sense of freedom that come from being free from worry—qualities happy people almost always have, even when they're busy.

Once Mohandas Gandhi was asked, "You have been working at least 15 hours a day, every day, for almost 50 years. Don't you think it's time for a vacation?"

Gandhi replied, "I am always on vacation."

Does Status Increase Happiness?

Social status is alluring. Throughout history, people have believed that they could fight their fear of not being enough by rising in the social hierarchy.

But status is a slippery slope. No matter how high you climb, there are countless people still above you. And there's always a long way to fall if your fortunes should fail. If you compare yourself to the people above you in the pecking order, you'll sabotage your self-esteem. If you allow yourself to feel superior to the people below you, you'll live in fear of dropping to their level.

Feeling superior to others is always tempting, but it's a terribly weak tool for achieving happiness. It may pamper your vanity but it will never bring you peace of mind. If status really made people happy, white-collar workers would be markedly happier than blue-collar workers, since they enjoy more status. As the graph below indicates, however, they're not.

Another interesting study showed that teenagers—who tend to be even more insecure and status-conscious than adults—are not happier

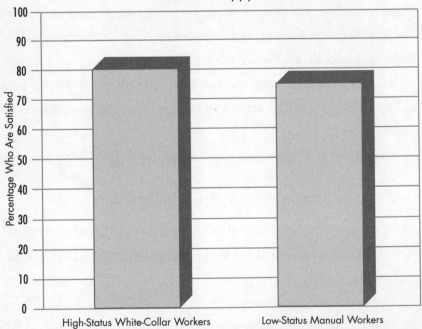

High-Status vs. Low-Status Workers
Percent "Happy with Life"

Ronald Inglehart, "Culture Shift in Advanced Industrial Society," copyright © 1990 by Princeton University Press. Reprinted by permission of Princeton University Press.

What Happy People Know

when they're reared in high-status families. In this study of 1,000 teenagers, those in the lower social classes reported the most happiness, and those in the highest social classes reported the least happiness. Rich kids usually have so much of everything that it's worth nothing. I call this *enriched deprivation*. Again, this might seem like one of those problems that you want to have, but it's not. Misery is misery.

One of the worst instigators of status seeking in our current culture is television, because of all its ads, and because so many people on TV are rich and beautiful. Among the most chilling studies on the effects of TV was one done shortly after it was introduced, in the 1950s. Because of government regulations, TV stations were first allowed to broadcast in just 34 cities in 1951, and then in 34 more cities in 1955. In 1951, in the first 34 cities in which TV was allowed, the rate of petty theft and larceny increased dramatically. Then, in 1955, the same increase in property crime was experienced in the next 34 cities. Researchers concluded that TV hyped material status so flagrantly that people became willing to steal to achieve it.

Furthermore, researchers noted that TV increased not only the desire for material status, but also the expectation of it. People felt they deserved status symbols after seeing people on TV with them.

This expectation of status pointed out an important general principle in the science of happiness: Happiness depends to a significant degree upon expectations. If you inflate your expectations, you're begging to be unhappy. That's one of the worst problems with wealth—it always bloats expectation. Rich people whine about things that would delight most people.

Happy people keep their expectations under constraint, no matter how much money they have. And they don't buy status symbols. They realize that materialistic status seeking is a weakness indulged in by insecure people, who are afraid to look inside themselves and face their true fears.

Happy people get their status from within. Their status symbols are things like a happy family, good friends, and pride in their work.

Do Possessions Increase Happiness?

If possessions were a reliable source of happiness, rich people would be significantly happier than middle-class people. But they're not. I see how true this is every day.

One of the regular guests at Canyon Ranch is a very nice but unhappy young woman from one of the wealthiest families of Australia. Her father has amassed several billion dollars developing skyscrapers all around the world, and he lavishes her with open-ended charge accounts and no-limit credit cards. She's addicted to shopping and binges on it like a junkie. It doesn't matter to her if she's buying a pair of $400 tennis shoes or a $100,000 antique vase—once she has the object of her desire in her sights, she's ravenous and unstoppable, a warrior princess on the prowl. But the moment she consummates her purchase, she always feels a huge letdown, one that goes way beyond buyer's remorse. Every purchase fails to fulfill her and makes her feel her fear of not being enough. For years, she's struggled to find a husband but hasn't been able to. She doesn't think she herself amounts to anything, so she's sure they just want her for her money. Even now, she's still trying to find someone to love her and is still grappling with her compulsion to spend. I can't honestly say that I've helped her. I wish all my clients were success stories, but that's just not how the world works. Not everybody gets it.

This woman's unhappiness might seem exotic—even absurd—but

it's common. One of the leading scientists in the study of happiness, Ed Diener, Ph.D., interviewed 49 of the wealthiest people in America and found that their happiness levels were only slightly above average. Eighty percent of these people agreed that wealth could make people unhappy.

The failure of material goods to make people happy is also seen in happiness studies of entire countries. Look at the chart below, "Happiness and Income in Economically Advanced Nations," and you'll see that among the world's economically advanced nations, the United States is one of the least happy countries even though it's by far the richest.

The same study that produced this chart, though, also showed that the very poorest countries in the world were also the least happy. This proves, again, that money *can* increase happiness when it relieves severe poverty.

Another fascinating chart on the relationship between money and happiness was compiled by preeminent happiness researcher Dr. David

HAPPINESS AND INCOME IN ECONOMICALLY ADVANCED NATIONS

Nation	Happiness Ranking	Income Index (compared to U.S.)
Switzerland	1st	4th
Denmark	2nd	19th
Canada	3rd	16th
Ireland	4th	48th
Netherlands	5th	24th
United States	6th	1st
Finland	7th	31st

Myers. This graph, below, tracks the rise of income in America since the 1950s. It shows that although income has risen dramatically, happiness has decreased somewhat since its peak in approximately 1965.

Here's one last, important thing to remember about happiness and possessions: There's a conspiracy out there—open and admitted—that's trying to convince you that you'll be happier if you buy various products. It's called consumerism, and it's the mainstay of every economy in the world, capitalistic or socialistic. In America, it accounts for about two-thirds of the economy. I'm all for a strong economy, but we've got to face

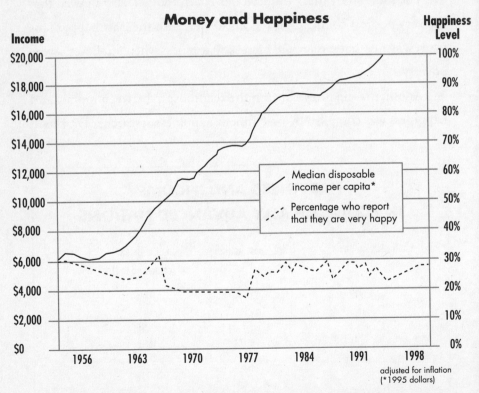

Money and Happiness

From David G. Myers, "The Funds, Friends, and Faith of Happy People," *American Psychologist*, vol. 55, No. 1, published by the American Psychological Association.

the fact that we're inundated each day with advertising messages that are designed to change the way we think. These messages are produced by some of the most creative, persuasive people in the world.

Be aware of the impact of these messages. Don't believe that happiness is in your next purchase. Think for yourself—or you'll never climb out of the money trap.

Does Financial Security Increase Happiness?

I often ask the guests of Canyon Ranch when they felt most happy. You'd think they'd say, "Right now," because the current moment usually marks the peak of their financial security. (It's true: The rich get richer, almost every day. That's simply the nature of wealth.) But they almost never say now. They usually talk about the past.

This tells me an important thing: Financial security doesn't increase happiness.

Last week I had an entrepreneur in my office, and I asked him when he'd been most happy. He started off telling me that he'd felt great a few months earlier, when he'd sold his start-up company for $700 million. But there was a hollow monotone in his voice that betrayed his lack of real satisfaction. So I prodded him to dig deeper and tell me when he'd truly felt happy, instead of when he should have felt happy. Then he started to rhapsodize about the most financially insecure time of his life, when he was just getting his company off the ground. Back then, he'd been eating macaroni and cheese every night, sleeping on a couch in his office, and fighting ferociously to make payroll every Friday. But he'd felt totally alive!

Now he was so fat with cash that he was building a $16 million house, but he complained that he just didn't have "the edge" that he once did—that raw, empowering feeling that comes when you've got nothing to lose.

Even more troubling to him, he still had the same old insecurities—about his looks, his father's opinion, and his health (he'd always been a hypochondriac—except in the early days of his business, when he'd been too busy to worry). He even worried about money more than ever, because he had so much of it to worry about! That paradox is common.

As he and I worked together over a period of about a week, he came to realize that financial security doesn't contribute much to happiness. It doesn't even provide the much more important feeling of personal security—feeling secure about who you are.

Even personal security, though, can be ephemeral. And complete security is a myth. No one feels totally secure, and no one should. We're all too vulnerable and life is too uncertain. We all age, we all become ill, we all lose people we love. We all die. These are the real insecurities of life, and neither money nor anything else can do a thing to stop them.

Financial security is fine. But it's not the path to happiness.

I never really realized quite how true that was, though, until I met one of my favorite guests of the Ranch, Linda Richman. Linda's life had been hard; she had lost a son and had spent 11 years in her house as a prisoner of agoraphobia. But she has great courage and an incredible sense of humor, and vaulted past her difficulties to become a big success. She went from being a guest at the Ranch to being one of its most popular lecturers, wrote the book *I'd Rather Laugh*, and has appeared on many national TV shows. She even became a major cult celebrity when she was parodied in the *Saturday Night Live* "Coffee Talk" sketch. Linda Richman does not have to worry about money.

But she does! Once she became so panic-stricken about it while driving that she had to pull off the road. Unlike many people, though, she knew that it wasn't the voice of her accountant shrieking tales of woe to her subconscious—it was her reptile. So she just told herself, "I'm in the fear mode. Get out of it!" And she did. Hopped back into her car and drove away.

Linda knows that she'll always feel insecure about money—just like the rest of us—but there's no good reason to suffer from it. Happy people have the courage to embrace their insecurity. They know it will always be there—as long as mankind is mortal—and that to experience it is to feel the true, rough essence of real life.

Does Worldly Power Increase Happiness?

The most powerful man I've ever known—a high-ranking federal official who has been a household name for about 20 years—once told me this about power: "The only people who are power-hungry are those who don't have any." Once you attain power, it becomes, as he put it, "a loathsome burden." When he said that, he looked a hundred years old.

He likened high political office to having a dozen children. Sure, you've got power over a lot of people, but it doesn't make you feel omnipotent—it makes you feel tired. Obligated. Responsible.

There are some people who derive pleasure from ordering others around, but they're just insecure people who have no real personal power: power over their own lives. People who run their own lives don't need to run others'.

Ironically, though, as people rise in worldly power, they often lose power over their own lives, because they've got so many people to please and obligations to meet. When this happens, reasonable people can become Little Hitlers. Sometimes they stay like that until they find a way to again manage their own lives.

Frequently, when people lose power over their own lives, they begin to tyrannize themselves with perfectionism. Perfectionism, like workaholism, is one of those vices that masquerades as a virtue—it's fear disguised as strength. I've had people sit in my office and congratulate themselves on their perfectionism even when it was killing them by contributing to their cardiovascular disease. Successful people, in particular, often swallow the myth that it's their perfectionism that has put them on top, rather than their brains and passion. One reason they feed themselves this myth is because perfectionism is so difficult that they need to exaggerate its benefits in order to be motivated to maintain it.

The popular clinical psychology perspective on perfectionism is that it's initiated by demanding parents. I disagree with this conventional, blame-the-parents explanation. I think perfectionism is just another mask for the fear of not being enough. It's for insecure people who think that only the most perfect among us will prevail.

Similar to perfectionism, and just as self-destructive, is obsession with control. People with money often think it should give them control over other people and their own lives, but it doesn't. In fact, control is a myth. Control connotes absolute power, and in this world, there's no such thing. I've seen countless people waste their lives struggling for control, and the more they demanded it, the further they fell from true power. True power comes from management, not control. Management means realizing that you can't control everybody and everything, and dealing with the world on its own terms—giving a little, taking a little. It *works*.

If you really could control your life, you'd never get sick, never get old, never die. Never even get a traffic ticket. Well . . . life has other plans.

In fact, this is the one psychology book that won't tell you to take control of your life. Life itself has something to say about your life, whether you like it or not.

If you adopt management of your own life as a primary goal, you'll be able to participate in your own destiny. But if you squander your energy struggling for complete control, you'll lose the reins of management and become just another leaf in the wind.

Participation in your own destiny can help make you happy. But struggling for power cannot. Perfectionism cannot. Control cannot.

Unfortunately, millions of people toil their whole lives away in the pursuit of power, perfectionism, control, status, and possessions.

There's a word for these people: unhappy.

Breaking Free

This is what science tells us about money and happiness.

But what does your heart tell you? Does it say, "By gosh, you're right! I have enough money. I'm never going to worry about it again."

I hope not! That would be phony.

In the human mind, money is married to survival, and you will always be nagged by fear of money's scarcity, just as you will always be nagged by fear of the fate that survival holds off: death. Your heart should tell you to accept this fear.

This fear is branded into your brain—it's hardwired—and there's no way and no reason to get rid of it. It is you.

Accept it. It's time now.

Welcome it. Laugh at yourself. Forgive yourself. Rise to the height of your soaring spirit. And move on.

CHAPTER THREE

The Other Traps: Treading the Minefield

In the 1970s, when the people of my generation were coming of age as adults, many of us sincerely felt that we had found the path to happiness. In that antimaterialistic era, millions of people had extricated themselves from the money trap—no small feat!—and seemed to stand on the threshold of lives of meaning and joy.

To grasp the goal of happiness, we felt, we needed only to tie up a few loose ends: We needed to feel more fully the many pleasures of life, resolve our childhood traumas, overcome a few lingering weaknesses, and then just resolve to be happy, no matter what.

It seemed so simple. Some days, you could almost see happiness, shimmering in the distance.

But we were trapped and didn't know it: That was the trick of the traps. The traps seemed to promise happiness, and lured a generation down a deceitful path.

To our surprise, happiness never arrived. Finally, after years of struggle and years of pain, many people gave up on finding lives of purpose, freedom, and spirituality. Happiness began to seem like a fiction, a fantasy that young people ascribed to the old, and old people ascribed to the young. In the 1980s and 1990s, people began to drift back into the pursuit of money, and looked for status, possessions, and power to fill their emptiness.

They felt betrayed by their own youthful vision of happiness. They weren't betrayed. They were just tricked and trapped. But no trap is eternal in the face of the human spirit.

Let me tell you now about the other four traps that surround happiness, almost like a minefield. I'll let you in on their tricks. Then you'll be free again to follow your own heart to the life that has long been awaiting you.

Happiness Trap #2: Trying to Find Happiness through Pleasure

"I've been up so long it looks like down to me," the movie star slurred, with a bad-boy grin as crooked as sin. The same lopsided grin had made him millions onscreen, but now was mirthless. He was describing the binge he was on, a Mardi Gras of alcohol, sex, and drugs that had left his eyes a soupy yellow.

He was a walking illustration of one of the new theories of the science of happiness. It's called adaptation level theory, and it says that once we become accustomed to any pleasure, it no longer has the power to make us happy.

This principle is one of the biggest obstacles to happiness that many people now face, because as a prosperous society we're awash in a sea of pleasures that were once out of reach. Average people today have more creature comforts than Louis XIV had.

Happy people, however, know that it's wise to regularly back away from life's banquet, so that pleasure will stay novel and refreshing. Unhappy people, including this film star, dive headlong into pleasure and try to wring every drop of gratification from it.

This doesn't work. Neurologically, it overloads the brain's pleasure centers, prohibiting further sensations, and depletes the feel-good neurotransmitters serotonin and dopamine. Psychologically, it creates inflated expectations and a sense of boredom. Physically, overindulgence in recreational substances, and even food, creates tolerance and addiction. Because of these factors, people who try to find happiness through pleasure soon end up trudging what researchers call the hedonic treadmill.

Even worse, these people also fall victim to a well-proven theory called the opponent process principle, which says that feelings tend to naturally trigger their opposites. This theory explains why people who observe a tragedy often feel elated afterward, or why people suddenly become sad at happy events, such as weddings. Plato noted this rebound effect long ago when he wrote, "How strange would appear to be this thing that men call pleasure! And how curiously it is related to what is thought to be its opposite, pain! Wherever the one is found, the other follows up behind."

The rebound effect was pounding my movie star client into the ground. He was sick, toxic, and jaded—but still convinced that he was seizing the moment and living life to the fullest. He thought the only reason everyone didn't live like him was because they didn't have the chance.

I appealed to his vanity—never the wrong strategy with Hollywood people. I challenged him to sober up during his week at the Ranch, and see me every day.

Over the next week, without his defensive pleasures to hide behind, he found another side of himself, one filled with spiritual hunger and fear. I told him that the happiness tools could fulfill his spiritual yearning and give him a healthy way to rise above his fears. But I warned him that if he couldn't climb out of the pleasure trap, it would eventually kill him—artistically, spiritually, and physically.

The end of the week came quickly, and when he left I was still worried about him. For him, staying sick would be so easy. His entourage liked him just the way he was. And the pressures of his career provided him with plenty of things to fear.

But he came through. He embraced the happiness tools and gradually began to understand his fears. The tools helped him lay off drugs and alcohol—not by forbidding them, but by healing the pain in his soul that he'd used the substances to soothe.

Pleasure, I have found, is uniquely effective at masking fear. Like the feeling of love, it preoccupies the brain in a positive way, prohibiting it from focusing upon fear. However, love can be sustained, while pleasure is notoriously transitory.

People have been using pleasure as a force against fear since the beginning of civilization. In the earliest years of human history, though, when life was short and threats were everywhere, pleasure was reserved primarily for times of celebration, such as the end of a hunt or a triumph over an enemy. The primary pleasures back then, as now, were feasting, use of intoxicants, dancing, music, stories, and sex. Thus, these pleasures came to be closely associated with safety and security.

Among happy people today, pleasure is still reserved for celebration. Happy people celebrate small achievements, such as finishing a day's work, with small pleasures, such as a cold beer or a good meal. They celebrate more important occasions, such as holidays, with greater indulgences.

During these pleasant interludes, they forget their fears, relax, and recharge their batteries. But they don't get trapped by what Ernest Hemingway called "the festival theory of life." They know that pleasures are merely the punctuation marks of life.

Happy people know that much of the good feeling that comes from pleasure is due to its dampening effect upon fear and anxiety, rather than from the physical sensation itself. Therefore, they tend to ritualize their pleasures, drawing contentment from the entire ritual, not just from the few moments of pure pleasure. For example, they might enjoy a cocktail hour by meeting at a favorite place with a few good friends, and savoring the entire experience—even if they have only half a glass of wine—instead of trying to toss down as much booze as possible.

Unhappy people stay too long at the party and end up celebrating celebration—indulging in pleasure for its own sake. When this happens, they blot out not only fear, but life itself, including the higher brain functions of the spirit and intellect. They fall into a lifeless trance and indulge robotically, losing track of what they're doing to their bodies and to the people around them. For a short time, they're free from fear. But when they return to normal life, they're saddled with guilt, toxicity, and heightened physical addiction. Then they often leap right back into pleasure—hair of the dog therapy—to soften the pain of overindulgence.

If you have a socially acceptable indulgence—such as lying in a recliner, watching movies, and eating—you might be thinking, "*I'm* not caught in the pleasure trap! My pleasures are wholesome." Think again. The most benign pleasures are often the most seductive, and can still be deadly to mind and body. Sixty thousand Americans die each year from illegal drugs, but at least 250,000 die from overeating and being sedentary. Before they die, these quarter million people often suffer terribly. This is a big price to pay for a happiness strategy that doesn't even work!

My friend and colleague Dr. Martin Seligman once did a fascinating exercise in which he asked a group of students to engage in two acts, one pleasurable and one altruistic. Virtually all of the students reported that the altruistic act made them happier than the pleasurable act. After the altruistic act, the rest of the day went better for almost all of them. But the good feeling from the pleasurable act faded as soon as it was over.

Pleasure is a good thing. But it is the dessert of life, not the meal.

Happiness Trap #3: Trying to Be Happy by Resolving the Past

Modern neuroscience, I believe, has found the subconscious. It is the amygdala.

The amygdala, as you may recall, is the portion of the brain, located in the limbic system, that is the storage facility for negative memories. It evolved about a million years ago as part of the hardwired warning system for danger. When early man saw a ripple of tall grass moving toward him on the savannah, it was his amygdala that told him that the ripple was a tiger.

About 100 years ago, Freud noted that people often stored traumatic memories beneath the surface of their day-to-day consciousness. Lacking the knowledge we now have of brain anatomy, he dubbed this black box of memory the subconscious, and theorized that if the box were to be cathartically emptied by means of psychoanalysis, people would no longer be haunted by traumatic events.

This theory became the foundation of clinical psychology. Psychologists began to promise their patients that if they could simply remember the events that had hurt them—particularly during childhood—they could rid themselves of neurosis and psychosis. This model of cathartic treatment meshed well with the still-developing field of modern medicine, because the fundamental goal of medicine at that time was to isolate the single, discrete causative factors of disease—bacteria, viruses, and other pathogens—and drive them from the body.

After World War II, when thousands of traumatized former soldiers besieged the Veterans Administration, this approach to psychology became firmly institutionalized. Millions of federal dollars were poured into helping soldiers recover from their wartime traumas. As in modern medicine, the emphasis was on relieving symptoms and helping people to become functional.

In that difficult era, little attention was paid to helping people rise above mere normalcy. In medicine, doctors focused almost solely upon eradicating illness—instead of helping patients achieve robust, elevated health—and in psychology, doctors focused almost exclusively on overcoming neurosis and psychosis, instead of helping patients achieve happiness and fulfillment.

In both disciplines, health was considered to be the mere absence of disease.

But health is more than that. Physical health is feeling great. And mental health is feeling happy. These days, the strongest new trend in medicine is to help patients achieve vigorous health, and the strongest new trend in psychology is to help people feel happy.

As this trend in medicine has accelerated, doctors have found, ironically, that building health is often the best way to defeat illness. Similarly, as the same approach has gained steam in psychology, psychologists have discovered that helping people become happy—without fixating on their anguish—usually solves mental problems even better than fighting the problems directly.

One of the main reasons that this approach is working so well in psychology is because Freud's basic premise was faulty. The subconscious cannot be emptied of its dark and dreadful contents merely by bringing them to the light of day. The subconscious, instead, is a living, functioning part of the brain—the amygdala—which cannot be drained. Freud's approach was mechanistic, but people aren't machines.

Furthermore, the brain stem, or reptilian brain, is also filled with instinctual and primordial fears that cannot be excised. A memory is a memory is a memory—and there's no healthy way to erase it. Whether memories are good or bad, they remain a part of you for as long as you live.

Because the most fundamental premise of traditional clinical psychology is faulty, the conventional mental health care system has not achieved satisfactory results. It's widely estimated that approximately

The Real Reasons Why People Recover in Therapy

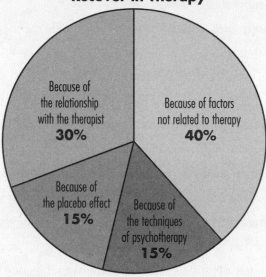

Because of
the relationship
with the therapist
30%

Because of factors
not related to therapy
40%

Because of
the placebo effect
15%

Because of
the techniques
of psychotherapy
15%

two-thirds of all psychological patients fail to improve. Furthermore, when patients do get better, it's usually not due to one or another of the basic techniques of conventional clinical psychology, such as counseling, biofeedback, hypnosis, or systematic desensitization. More frequently, positive changes occur in patients because of (1) factors that are not related to therapy, (2) the patient's relationship with a supportive therapist, or (3) the placebo effect. These factors were quantified, according to a meta-analysis of numerous studies, in the interesting pie graph shown above.

In fact, some cathartic therapies that are designed to release subconscious angst do more harm than good. A recent Iowa State University study revealed that conventional cathartic therapy used for anger management tended to actually make people more prone to aggression.

Unfortunately, several generations of Americans have been led to believe that the only way clinical psychology can help them is by dredging up their traumatic memories. Millions have tried this—and most have not been helped. Because of this, the reputation of clinical psychology has been tarnished. Legions of people are now convinced that it consists of little more than touchy-feely psychobabble that never changes anything.

There's a better way. It's transcendence. Even though your black box of fears and traumas—your amygdala—will always be in your brain, you can transcend its pain. You can rise above it by funneling your mental energy into your spirit and intellect. Your powers of intellect and spirit can create new meaning out of old memories.

Your painful memories, which may once have made you feel like a victim—battered and demeaned—can become your greatest motivators and your richest sources of wisdom.

Let me tell you about a guest at the Ranch who achieved that.

He was referred to me by a psychiatrist who thought he needed counseling reinforcement to begin a regimen of Prozac. The guest, Rick, was suffering from major depression, triggered by the death of his wife after an excruciating illness.

For half an hour, I let Rick, who really had been through hell, pour out his guts to me. A little catharsis is a good thing; it opens the wound and lets you see what's needed for healing.

Rick, it seems, had met his wife, Mona, in one of those magical moments in which the chemistry just clicks. They were perfect for each other, and the first years of their relationship were idyllic. But then, seemingly out of nowhere, Mona developed heart disease, and was in and out of intensive care many times. For years, she clung to life, and he was with her every moment, caring for her physically and emotionally. Many surgeries were required, including amputations of limbs, and when she died she weighed 35 pounds. By then, Rick was spent. A ghost.

My heart was in pain just hearing about it.

I asked Rick a constructive question. That's a technique I'll soon teach you that lights the way to positive action. It was important for Rick to take action, because talk was never going to pull him out of the life story he was stuck in: "I'm a tragic victim of love lost." One of the worst things about the Freudian approach is that it makes people think they can just talk a problem to death, without actually having to do anything.

The constructive question some people might have asked Rick was, "Don't you think Mona would have wanted for you to move on and be happy?" But that was too self-centered for Rick. He was a giver, not a taker. He would've balked. So I asked, "If the situation were reversed, and you had died, what would you want Mona to do?"

Well, by God, he said, he would have wanted her to go out and have a full life. That was the kind of relationship they had.

"If that's the case, what do you think your role in that relationship should be now?"

It was as if I'd shaken him awake. When you rouse someone's own inner wisdom, it doesn't take long to help them heal.

Slowly, but with a strong voice, he said, "You know what? I've been feeling sorry for myself. For far too long. Mona and I hate it when people feel sorry for themselves." Even though he had tears in his eyes, he began to tell me about all the changes he was going to make. He was going to see his family more, join a church, go hunting and fishing, join a bowling league. On and on.

When Rick walked out after that hour, it was as if there was new blood in him, new air, new life.

The doctor who'd referred him to me called me back the next day. Worried. "Today he's so full of energy, he's manic," the doctor said. "He must be bipolar. Forget the Prozac. Let's try lithium."

Rick never took the lithium, or the Prozac. He did all the things he said he would, and the next time we talked, he had a new life story. It was: "I had more love in a few short years than most people have in a lifetime."

His pain was still there. It always would be. It had happened, and nothing could change that.

But his spirit had soared, and his reptile had ceased to rule.

That's not resolution. How can you resolve what he'd suffered?

It's transcendence—and it's one of the true paths to happiness.

Happiness Trap #4: Trying to Be Happy by Overcoming Weaknesses

The lore of psychotherapy and the literature of self-help is permeated with the idea that people can overcome their weaknesses. So it must be true, right?

Well . . . to be brutally honest, I haven't seen much of that in my 30 years of practice.

I see people changing their lives every day—but it's not by correcting their weaknesses. It's by building their strengths.

For example, I've helped a number of alcoholics to stop drinking. Does that mean they no longer have a weakness for alcohol? God, no!

They obviously have a weakness for it—that's why they can't touch it. But their continued sobriety tells me that they also have a set of strengths that overrides that weakness.

Trying to cure weaknesses is a waste of the energy that's needed to achieve change. People often spend their lifetimes waging war on their weaknesses, and still die with the same foibles they've always had.

Trying to overcome weaknesses may sound heroic, but it's really just another way of being reactive to fear, instead of being proactive about making life better.

When people give in to the automatic fear reaction and take the road that leads them away from their intellects and spirits, they invariably begin to focus on everything that's negative in their lives and personalities. They fixate on correcting their weaknesses. But focusing on weaknesses, like focusing on anything else that's negative, just reinforces fear. It limits your options to the sparse menu of the fear response: fighting, fleeing, and freezing.

Especially intractable are socially approved weaknesses. The most notorious of these in our society is the weakness of workaholism. People who would be ashamed to admit that they are alcoholics or drug addicts often boast about being workaholics. Other weaknesses that are disguised as strengths include perfectionism, stoicism, materialistic ambition, desire for domination, and status seeking.

At one point in my career, I specialized in the psychology of stress and cardiovascular disease, and met a multitude of people with socially encouraged weaknesses. Many had destroyed their cardiovascular systems with their fixations on money, control, and status. In the hospital, I heard the horror stories of these people. They were driven by fear, obsessed with time, and completely focused on doing instead of being.

Their fears of not having enough and not being enough had landed them in Cardiac Rehab, frantically bargaining with God for another chance.

The best way to help these people was not to deny them their weaknesses. That was just self-defeating and punishing—a waste of their healing energy. Instead, I encouraged them to focus on their strengths, such as being good parents, being socially active, or enjoying sports. That soothed their fears and activated their neocortical responses. It reduced weaknesses like workaholism and perfectionism, but in a fun, positive way.

Focusing on strengths works simply because it feels better than focusing on weakness. It creates energy, which is always necessary for transformation. Also, it's self-sustaining and it's full of rewards. My high-school football coach used to tell us, "Don't play not to lose. Play to win. It works better."

Long ago, psychology pioneer B. F. Skinner found that people could be reliably conditioned to act in certain ways when he applied a system of rewards and punishments. One of the most important things he discovered was that rewards (or positive conditioning) were far more powerful than punishments (or negative conditioning).

I first discovered the futility of trying to reverse weaknesses in the late 1970s, when I began working with a teenage girl who had a serious eating disorder. At first, as other psychologists had, I confronted her weakness regarding food. I tried to talk some sense into her. But she just dug in her heels. She was frozen with fear, and I got nowhere. But I couldn't afford to stay nowhere, because this poor girl, Bonnie, was drawing close to death.

I still remember the day we had to insert a feeding tube into her. As Bonnie watched her sunken stomach begin to distend slightly from the nutrition that was being pumped into it, she became hysterical. "I'm getting fat!" she shrieked.

She was actually near a terminal point of starvation. Months before, she'd stopped eating red meat, and then had removed any kind of meat or fish from her diet. After that, she'd stopped eating bread, cereal—all grains. It hadn't been enough. She'd stopped eating heavy vegetables, such as potatoes and beans, and then had eliminated salads. Two days previously, she'd stopped drinking water. Too fattening. She'd ended up in the hospital with severe dehydration.

As nutrients and fluids began to form a tiny bulge against the thin skin of her abdomen, she looked horrified. "I'm a blimp!" she cried, searching my face for pity.

I didn't try to contradict her, because the fantasy of fatness that this 88-pound high school student had created for herself was as real to her as the hospital bed in which she was lying.

As I got to know Bonnie, I struggled to find a way to help her write a new story of her life. The better I got to know her, the more I realized that the story she was telling herself—"fat and gross"—was just a reflection of her fear, made real by her mind. Interestingly, that wasn't even her worst fear. Her worst fear was that she was, as she put it, "a human zero"—nothing but "a crummy student" and "a loudmouth." Her fear of being overweight was just a substitute fear. Her real fear was of not being enough—and she hated herself for it.

Even at that early stage in my career, I intuitively knew—it was just common sense—that the best cure for hate was love.

Therefore, I asked Bonnie what she loved most in the world, and she told me it was her little dog, Rover Reddy. So when Bonnie was strong enough to get out of bed, I arranged to have Rover Reddy brought to the hospital. It freaked out the administration, but so what? Bonnie's relationship with her dog was one of her few remaining strengths, and I wanted to build on it.

One day, while she was cuddling Rover Reddy, I asked her how she felt about him.

"I love him," she said.

"Love him how?"

"Like I want to take care of him."

"Would you starve him?"

"No!" She looked at me as though I were crazy. Then she suddenly understood what I was getting at, and I could almost see her look inward. That was the foothold, the beginning of her recovery.

I let her play with the dog as much as she wanted, and she gradually began to see that her dog was not only her pet, but was also part of her own selfhood—and that the dog was certainly good enough, and so was she. She found that she did love herself, just as she loved her dog. We talked a great deal about her good points and all of her strengths. And we completely ignored her obsessive ideas about food. Food didn't matter to me. Bonnie mattered.

When Bonnie's love for herself began to grow, her fear subsided, and the language she used to describe her life began to change. It didn't happen overnight; it happened in increments, as most healing does. After a few months, though, she was no longer a "crummy student"; she was someone who had "trouble in a couple of classes." She wasn't a "loudmouth," but someone who was "not afraid to speak my mind." Her body was no longer "fat and gross," but was just "more womanly."

Bonnie was rewriting her life story. She not only wrote a fresh, healthy version of her current life, but also her past. The facts of her life were unchanged—after all, a memory is a memory, and reality is reality—but what those memories and that reality *meant* had changed completely. Bonnie had not merely accepted the past or grown to understand it, but had actually rewritten its history.

Since then, I've seen this happen many times. Nothing is written in stone—not even what has already happened.

Bonnie's anorexia diminished, and then vanished—without her ever confronting it head-on. Bonnie went on to college, played sports, fell in love, and found happiness—without ever looking for it.

For the first time, I'd seen that when I could help people to find their strengths, they didn't need to go to war against their weakness.

A little later, I became founding director of the Eating Disorders Program at the University of Nebraska School of Medicine, and worked with many more girls who had anorexia. By then, I knew better than to confront their weaknesses. I never talked about eating with them. They weren't good at eating. I talked about what they *were* good at and about what they loved.

Then, when they finally found their strengths, they began to nourish their newfound selves.

Happiness Trap #5: Trying to Force Happiness

Abraham Lincoln once said, "People can be just about as happy as they make up their minds to be."

Oh? If that's true, why did Lincoln dose himself with a crude antidepressant, mercury tablets (which made him fly into rages)? Why was his wife suicidally depressed?

You can't just decide to be happy any more than you can decide to be taller.

That's because happiness is not a finite entity unto itself, but is the sum of the 12 most important qualities of happiness: love, optimism, courage, a sense of freedom, proactivity, security, health, spirituality, altruism, perspective, humor, and purpose. These are the things you should make up your mind to achieve.

Of course, achieving these qualities is tough. But that's the point! Happiness isn't la-la land. It's not for the weak or lazy. If you wanted to become physically fit, you wouldn't expect to get there by just deciding, would you? When people try to be happy by just resolving to be, happiness becomes a mirage, forever fading into the distance.

Happiness is hard work—and it's harder for some people than others, because there is a genetic component to it. In an important study of identical twins who were reared in different homes, it was found that happiness may be as much as 40 percent heritable. In this study, identical twins who were reared apart were found to be more likely to have the same happiness levels than nonidentical twins who were raised in the same home. This study shows why it's especially important for people who are not genetically predisposed to happiness to use the happiness tools.

Fortunately, most of the 12 major qualities of happiness—such as love, optimism, and freedom—are intrinsically pleasant, and most of the happiness tools that help generate these elements are innately satisfying.

For example, one of the simplest and most effective things you can do to lift your mood is to simply keep a pleasant expression on your face. This was proven in a study in which half the subjects were asked to hold pens in their teeth—which made their expressions approximate a smile—while the other subjects held pens in their lips, which created pouts. Both groups were told a series of jokes. The group with the pens in their teeth rated the jokes as funnier.

Now you know the key to happiness. Hold a pen in your teeth.

Better yet, use the happiness tools.

The tools are all about action. If you could just force yourself to be happy, through sheer willpower—without doing anything—you wouldn't need the tools. I've seen people try to do this. But it doesn't work.

Fear is just too strong. Fear, fear, endless fear.

Think about these things: racial tension, tribal clashes, religious hostility. Office politics, backstabbing, sexual conflict. Gang violence. International strife. Jealousy, greed, hate, intolerance, war. They all stem, at the core, from fear. Fear of not having enough. Fear of people who are different. Fear of domination. Fear of not being enough. Fear of ideas. Fear of love. Fear of death. Fear of life.

And how much of it makes sense? How much is reasonable? Inevitable? None of it. I swear to God, none of it.

If we could just rise above fear . . . what a world we would have.

It's time to try.

Start by yourself. That's the only way anything ever begins.

Learn the happiness tools. They can change your life. They've worked for others. Now it's your turn.

CHAPTER FOUR

The Antidote
to Fear

I saw a happy man today—someone who was vibrant with life. He was on television, and he was so luminous with vitality that he seemed to leap right off the screen.

He said that he had the greatest job in the world, and just looking at him, you couldn't possibly doubt it. He was a firefighter, one who had just come off duty, and his helmet was still ashen and grimy, but he wore it like a crown.

"We love what we do!" he was enthusing to a reporter, plainly proud

79

and rightfully so. "We're the guys who are running in while everybody else is running out."

I was struck by that expression, and by the joy he reflected when he said it. It's a perfect metaphor for the kind of people we all need to be, if we're ever going to be truly happy. We need to be willing to charge headlong into the inferno of our most horrific fears—eyes open, intellect and spirit at the ready—even as our survival instincts are screaming, "Run! Run! Get out!"

That takes courage, and that's why courage is one of the prerequisites for happiness.

Courage, they say, is not the lack of fear, but the ability to take action in spite of it. But where does that ability come from? What power grants the strength to overcome the sick, shaky feeling of fear?

Only one power is that strong: love.

In the ultimate analysis, human beings have only two essential, primal feelings: fear and love. Fear impels us to survive, and love enables us to thrive. This complementary pair of feelings has been the driving force of human history.

Fear is the product of the reptilian brain, hardwired into every fiber of our being, and love is the product of the neocortical higher brain, where spirit and intellect reside. Thus, the dance of the spirit and reptile—the shifting balance between the neocortex and the reptilian brain—is the dance of love and fear.

For you to be happy, love must lead this dance.

Love, though, for all we talk about it, is still an amorphous term with many meanings, some quite contradictory. Some people, for example, equate love with a feeling of longing, while others see it as satisfaction. Love can mean romantic love, or, quite differently, the love of a parent for a child. For that matter, the love of a parent for a child varies greatly from the love of a child for a parent. Children need, and parents need to be needed—and yet both call it love.

In the struggle for happiness, however, there is only one special quality of love that really matters. That element of love is appreciation.

Appreciation is the highest, purest form of love. It is the type of love that can blossom even when it is not returned. It is the outward-bound, self-renewing form of love that has no dependence upon romantic attachment or family ties. People who truly appreciate feel the same about the object of their appreciation whether it is present or absent. They appreciate it even if it is, by objective standards, not worthy of their appreciation. Appreciation asks for nothing, and gives everything.

When you enter into the active condition of appreciation—whether over something as common as a sunset or as profound as the love in your child's eyes—your normal world stops and a state of grace begins. Time can stand still, or rush like a waterfall. Your senses can be heightened or obliterated. Creativity flows, heart rate slows, brain waves soften into rolling ripples, and an exquisite calm descends over your entire being. During active appreciation, your brain, heart, and endocrine system work in synchrony and heal in harmony.

Most important of all, during active appreciation, the threatening messages from your amygdala and the anxious instincts of your brainstem are cut off, suddenly and surely, from access to your brain's neocortex, where they can fester, replicate themselves, and turn your stream of thoughts into a cold river of dread.

It is a fact of neurology that the brain cannot be in a state of appreciation and a state of fear at the same time. The two states may alternate, but are mutually exclusive.

A somewhat similar neurological phenomenon also helps protect you from physical pain. When you bruise yourself, you instinctively rub the fresh injury to help stop the pain. It works because touch signals travel to the brain almost 10 times faster than pain signals, and the brain can only process one set of signals at a time.

By the same token, when you create a state of appreciation, through activation of the intellect and spirit, you are free from fear during that time.

Thus, appreciation is the antidote to fear.

Because fear is the greatest enemy of happiness, appreciation is the most important of the six major happiness tools. It is the source that gives power to the other tools.

Appreciation is surely the wellspring of the courage that enables fire-fighters to run into burning buildings while everyone else is running out. What else could possibly empower them to do it, again and again? Not glory. Certainly not money. Not even obligation. There's only one thing that could realistically account for it: In their hearts, there must certainly be a deep appreciation for life in general, and for other people in partic-ular. This love, as much as their physical bravery, is the reason we regard them as heroes.

It was appreciation that enabled my father to do an equally dan-gerous job during World War II. Dad had an extraordinary love of life and appreciation for people, and it gave him the peace of mind and op-timism he needed to be able to defuse bombs. During the London blitz, he straddled 500-pound bombs that had landed but not exploded, and delicately disarmed them. Not a job for a fearful person!

He had that ability that always comes with deep appreciation for life:

the ability to see the world as a good place—even when he was sitting on top of a bomb. He once told me that he was even grateful for the bombs' immense power: "If I made a mistake, I'd never know it."

That was his trump card against the horror of war, his own little joke, and he genuinely thought it was funny. To others, it would have been horrifying.

After the war, he kept his fearlessness about death. He sometimes said to me, when the subject came up, "Either you go to heaven or nothing happens at all—and how can you be scared of nothing?"

But people who don't love life are often afraid of nothingness—partly because it has already begun to pervade their lives.

Dad never ducked a mission, no matter how dangerous, mostly because of his love and appreciation for the other guys in his outfit. Military units have always been based on small, tightly bonded groups, the size of platoons, because leaders have always known that the strongest motivating force in the world is love of the people around you. It's the only force powerful enough to make people run out of trenches into gunfire or fall onto live hand grenades.

I'm sure you've experienced this same willingness to sacrifice for someone you deeply love. There may be no concept or ideal in existence that you would be brave enough to die for, but if you had to leap in front of a truck to save one of your kids, you'd probably do it in a heartbeat, and be grateful that you were there to help.

Only love is stronger than fear.

My father's fearlessness didn't fade even after he had a disabling stroke and was forced to live on in the shadow of death. The stroke left him unable to participate in the one activity he loved most, fishing for walleye in Lake Erie, and I was afraid this might drain away his love for life, and with it, his deep reservoir of courage. But without missing a beat he began to fish for bass in the small ponds of rural Ohio, and he grew to love that with a level of passion most people never experience.

My dad is much on my mind today, because he died recently.

I hate that he's dead. I'd give every penny I have to see him one more time, just to say good-bye.

But I have so much to appreciate, too. I love it that I had a dad who stomped this earth like a bull elk for 77 years, happy and unafraid, in his element. I'm fantastically lucky to have had a father who filled his life with meaning. The fulfillment that he showed me is possible—the path of fearless contentment that he walked—is my inheritance. It's worth a fortune to me. It's everything.

Of course, if I let myself, I could die a little bit inside from this, instead of finding a way to live even more. But . . . why?

The firefighter I saw on TV could have been diminished by his ordeal, rather than revitalized by it. Some people look into the face of death and spend the rest of their lives running. But not him.

Courage is always inspiring, but his was made more powerful by the unutterable grief that surrounded him. He was standing in the ruins of the World Trade Center.

Since the tragedy of 9/11, more people than ever have been visiting me and calling me. Most of them are former guests of the Ranch who live in Manhattan or have family there, and their pain is stark. They have so much to mourn.

But my father and this firefighter—brave men, both—tell us, one with his proud voice and one with his living spirit, that there is always more, even in the deepest grief, to love than to fear.

And so we continue, using love to find courage, and courage to find love, with tragedy certain in our mortal lives—and happiness as possible as ever.

What Tragedy Can Teach

I haven't always been able to find joy in times of sorrow. Like all sons, I should have learned more from my father than I did.

Instead, I learned to be positive and optimistic the only way that I think you can learn it—the hard way. Ironically, you can't learn optimism when things always go right. That only teaches complacency.

Complacency is a house of cards, because if life teaches us anything, it's that problems and loss are inevitable. Happiness isn't the art of building a trouble-free life. It's the art of responding well when trouble strikes.

My own heartbreak struck early. I was young and in love, a doctor of psychology on the way up, just starting a family, and feeling more or less invulnerable. Then my world fell apart.

I was having the happiest day of my life. My second son was born, and he was soft and tiny and adorable. I saw the family resemblance, and it was like discovering gold. I saw his whole life stretching ahead of him—his infancy, his toddler years, childhood, college, beyond—and it made my own life seem so much happier and more connected to the world. When I held little Ryan, he felt like love incarnate in my arms. And then the doctor said, "Something's not right."

My feet got cold and I could feel my heart kick against my chest as the doctor began to try to stimulate Ryan's breathing.

A little later, as Ryan wiggled fitfully in an incubator behind a thick wall of glass, the doctor told me in a tight voice that Ryan appeared to have hyaline membrane syndrome, a failure of the lung's alveolar sacs. The hospital wasn't equipped to deal with it, so Ryan was loaded into an ambulance to take him to the larger city of Lincoln, Nebraska.

The memory of that ambulance, red lights flashing in the black night, is burned into my brain.

We did everything we could, including praying, of course, but little Ryan died.

Because my wife was still in the hospital recovering from the C-section birth, I had to attend to the details of death by myself—looking in the Yellow Pages for a funeral home, selecting a plot that was somehow appropriate, picking out a tiny casket, and buying a headstone and trying to think of what to say on it. What can you say?

Take my word for it: Your worst memories will never fade.

I bottomed out on grief. Even now, as sick as my heart is with the loss of my dad, I know that nothing can touch the despair that tortured me then. I was inconsolable, afraid to start each day and even more afraid of the endless future, totally impotent to rescue my emotions from a feeling of sinking, sinking, sinking.

I asked God, "Why me?" and every time I seemed to get an answer, I argued against it. No, we hadn't scheduled the delivery too early. No, it hadn't been my fault that the small hospital couldn't help him. No, it wasn't genetic. No, I hadn't done something so evil that I deserved this. I wrestled with God—but that's a fight you never win.

Because my life continued, whether I liked it or not, I tried to piece

What Happy People Know

my world back together. But as most people do—even young psycholo-gists who are supposed to know better—I tried to find my world again by using coping mechanisms that did more harm than good. At the time, they seemed reasonable, even courageous. I've learned since then, though, that the coping mechanisms I was using just make the prison walls of grief and fear stronger. These days, I even have a pejorative name for these maladaptive coping mechanisms: the Dirty Ds. As I struggled to survive emotionally, I *demanded* that my fate be altered, even though no alteration could possibly suffice. When not enough happened, I *de-valued* my efforts to recover, and sank deeper into helplessness. I began to *demean* myself and think that I somehow deserved this tragedy, through some weakness I wasn't wise enough to recognize. Instead of trying to learn from my loss, I *discarded* its lessons. I saw it as pain, and nothing else. And as failure piled upon failure, I *desperately doubled* all of my ill-conceived efforts, thinking that if I could just dump more of my heart and soul into this agony, I'd find a way out.

It didn't happen. The Dirty Ds will betray you every time. It's aston-ishing that they're so popular.

Then one day, when I couldn't stand the onslaught of even one more moment of morbid thoughts, I pretended for a few seconds, or maybe a minute or two, that Ryan was still with us, and I let myself love him as I had when I'd first held him in my arms.

For that short time, the darkness lifted. The oasis of denial was a comfort.

But, I wondered, was it really the denial that had done it? In my head, I knew all too well that my son was dead. So without this pretense, I again let myself focus on my love for him. And the respite from the pain returned.

Over time—a long time—I found that when I actively allowed myself to summon all my love for Ryan, I actually felt better—strange surprise—instead of worse.

I also found that I could love Ryan very much despite the fact that he would never love me back—never even know me. I realized that my love for him (and not his for me) was the legacy he'd left, and that no one could ever take it away. Except for me. And I refused to let go. The love was too powerful and too sweet. It was the one thing that was greater than the pain.

Every day, through tears at first, I set aside time to let myself rest in the tranquility of my love for my little boy. Gradually, the love I experienced began to grace me with more than just a vacation from pain. It also gave me the emotional power to forgive, and to stop torturing myself with the question, Why me? In an emotional holocaust like this, you can blame anybody and everybody—the doctors who should have known more, the ambulance driver who could have driven faster, the taxpayers who refused to build a bigger hospital. Myself. Fate. God.

But I forgave. I let go of my somehow comforting companionship with anger.

When I did this, I discovered that my anger was mostly just a substitute emotion for a much deeper pain that was even harder to handle. The deeper pain was fear—fear of having to live out the rest of my tarnished life with my son gone, and with fate and God against me.

The more I forgave, the more I came to my senses and realized that even though Ryan was gone, neither God nor anyone else had ever been against me, and that my fate was far from sealed.

The forgiveness blessed me with inner security and gave me an unexpected sense of personal power. I began to stop feeling as if my emotions depended mostly upon the actions of others and upon destiny itself. Life could batter me, but it couldn't make me hate anyone—not even myself.

I slowly gained strength, as one might after a battle with a terrible disease, and I became more able to reach out and help other people—my grieving family, my clients, my friends—and I got another shock. Giving of myself, even when I still felt I had to hoard my strength, brought in more vitality than it gave out. The more I emptied myself of my energy and my love for others, the more I felt myself begin to fill up again with life and hope.

There was more of the world outside of me, I found, than in.

And then one ordinary morning, with no fanfare, as is so often the case when real change occurs, I knew that there was new knowledge in me. It was the kind of liberating, no-illusions knowledge that only suffering can bring. I knew that my love for Ryan was mine forever, locked into my heart, immortal. I knew that no event could ever again devastate me so completely. I knew that life was precious and ephemeral, and that from here on, I would treasure my first son, Brett, even more that I had before. And I learned that if I focused on giving love to Ryan, my family, my friends, and my clients, I could be whole in my soul once more.

These lessons were of tremendous value to me. But I knew, even on that first morning, that I could never have learned them without suffering.

So on that otherwise ordinary day, I became an optimist. I learned what optimism really is: It's knowing that the more painful the event, the more profound the lesson.

There are so many lessons in this life that we just don't want to learn—lessons about how dangerous life can be and how vulnerable we all are. You can't just tell someone these things and expect him to become wise. Wisdom only comes the hard way. But when it comes, it can keep you from suffering even greater tragedies in the future, including the greatest tragedy of all, which is to waltz through life unaware, unconnected, and unfulfilled.

I had learned that no event, no matter how painful or destructive, is all bad.

I had learned optimism.

It was time for me to try to teach it.

The Impact of Love on the Body and Brain

At first, I assumed that I could teach the lessons I had learned to anyone who had suffered a terrible reversal in life. These people, I thought, would be open to new ways of coping.

I was wrong.

I found out how wrong I was when I became director of behavioral medicine at the National Center for Preventive and Stress Medicine, based in Phoenix. That title was a fancy way of saying I was the psychologist in charge of trying to keep people from killing themselves with their own thoughts.

Many of my clients in this program were Phase Three Cardiac Rehabilitation patients. In Phase One, they'd had a near-fatal heart attack and had been treated for it. In Phase Two, they'd gone home to recuperate. In Phase Three, they'd returned to the hospital to learn how to live a new type of life.

My job was to show them how to keep from destroying their hearts with fear and anger. That wasn't easy, because most of these people—almost all of them midlife males—were practically drowning in anxiety. Part of their fear, of course, came from standing on the precipice of death, but most of their fear had preceded, and helped to cause, their heart attacks.

We tend to forget, in this era of concern about cholesterol, that anxiety still appears to be the greatest single contributor to heart disease. Consider these facts.

◆ More than half of all cases of heart disease are not related to the common risk factors of high cholesterol, smoking, or inactivity. (*Integration of Physiology and Behavioral Science*, 1993, vol. 28)

◆ In a Mayo Clinic study of people with heart disease, emotional stress was the strongest single predictor of further problems, such as heart attack or cardiac arrest. (*Mayo Clinic Proceedings*, 1995, vol. 70)

◆ Three separate studies have shown that stress is more closely related to heart disease, and to cancer, than smoking is. (*British Journal of Medical Psychology*, 1988, vol. 61)

◆ A study conducted at Harvard showed that men who experience elevated chronic anxiety are six times more likely than contented men to die from a sudden heart attack. (*Circulation*, 1994, vol. 89)

In the Cardiac Rehab Unit, it was easy to see that fear was killing these guys, but it was hard to get them to do something about it. Some of them were virtually married to their fear, often because they thought it had been their major motivator for success. In effect, they were afraid *not* to be afraid. Money and status were very important to them. You wouldn't want to be a mugger sticking a gun in those guys' ribs and demanding, "Your money or your life"—they'd spend all day deciding.

I tried to get through to these men, but their general attitude was, "How much can I get away with and still survive?" They did their exercises grudgingly, they made faces when the dietician told them about low-fat eating, and their eyes glazed over when I tried to tell them there was more to life than money. They seemed to be thinking, "Give me one good reason why I should take advice from somebody making 32 grand a year."

But not everyone in Cardiac Rehab was like this. About one-third of the group came in every day looking as though they'd just won the lottery: They'd looked death in the eye—and survived! Hot damn! They threw themselves into their rehab routines and never looked back. Trade success for . . . life? God, yes! And thank you!

Every afternoon, all the Phase Three Rehab guys worked out on our various exercise machines, wearing Holter monitors to make sure their hearts didn't beat out of rhythm, and they informally sorted themselves into the two distinct groups—the one with pained expressions, and the other looking as if they'd seen the face of God (but didn't care to see it again for a few more decades). I came to think of the two groups as the Happy Guys, who were in love with life, and the Scared Guys, who just hated the idea of death.

One thing quickly became obvious: Virtually all of the Happy Guys were on the cusp of recovery, with ruddy cheeks, good endurance, and strong numbers on their cardiac health indices. But most of the Scared Guys were ghostly and tentative, with weak numbers.

I began to ask myself, What do the Happy Guys know?

I got an answer to that question one morning when I was counseling one of the few female participants in the program.

Her name was Marlene, and she wasn't in the program because of serious heart problems, even though she was 86. She was participating primarily because she was a member of our board of directors, and we were trying to keep them as informed as possible about our program. So Marlene worked out with us every afternoon, gravitating to the group of Happy Guys, who considered her a hero because of her grit and good humor. After all, if anybody was a short-timer in this life, it was she, but you'd never have known it by the way she acted. Marlene had arrived in Arizona before it was even a state, walking behind a covered wagon, and she had the proud spirit and resiliency that have always been this country's greatest resources.

When I first met her, I was still under the sway of conventional, blame-the-past cynical psychology, and I once made the mistake of going on too long about the death of her son in the Korean War. I figured she still needed to process it.

"Dr. Baker," she said firmly, "I'd rather focus on my living children, because I can still *do* something about them." Well! So much for processing, transference, and all the rest of it. Marlene knew something about life, and that always beats knowing something about psychology.

During the same conversation, when she spoke of her husband, dead for 20 years, her eyes went far away and soft-focused, and you could see her love, still there on her brave and lined face, never to fade. I said something along the lines of what a good man he must have been. No way, she said. He was a womanizer and a drunk. A real pain in the butt. "But we had more love than most people ever dream of," she said, still lost in the happiness of her love.

You can bet *that* gave me something to think about.

Here was this woman who could have been bitter and bereft—who should have been, by actuarial odds, dead. And yet she was still in the flower of life, still working, still abundantly appreciative: *happy*.

From that day on, I realized that there was something happy people know that unhappy people don't: No matter what happens in life, there's always something left to love, and the love that remains is always stronger than anything that goes against it.

That was the same knowledge that had saved me when Ryan died, and now I saw that it was a universal truth.

Not long after that, I lost Marlene. I'd known it was inevitable. Being around all those sick people was just a little too much for her.

She ran off to England and married her new boyfriend, a London cab driver whom she described as "funny as hell." He was only 76; it was one of those May-December romances.

I've never seen anyone happier than Marlene on the day she left for the airport. Now she had new love to add to the old. It gave her tremendous strength and unbounded optimism.

Putting Appreciation to Work for You

What I learned from Marlene, and from the group of Cardiac Rehab Happy Guys, meshed perfectly with not only what I'd learned from Ryan, but also with what I'd learned a few years earlier from the girls in my Eating Disorders Clinic. Those girls had shown me that the best way to overcome anorexia was not to go to war against the disorder, but to appreciate the girls' own positive qualities, so they wouldn't need to pursue "perfection" through anorexia.

A few other psychologists were coming to similar conclusions at about the same time, including my friend Dr. Martin Seligman, who later categorized this approach as *positive psychology*. These days, positive psychology is the strongest new movement in the field, but back then, we were all just stumbling toward discovery.

To some extent, I blazed my own trail when I combined positive psychology with my existing specialty, medical psychology. I became a positive medical psychologist, one of only a few practicing.

At that time, in the mid-1980s, most doctors were coming to realize that negative thoughts hurt the body. Only a small group of us, though, had begun to believe that positive thoughts heal the body—and even heal the mind of its own survival-based fear.

By now, though, that idea has been proven. Some of the best research has been done by my colleague Barbara Frederickson, Ph.D., of the University of Michigan. She has shown that positive emotions such as joy and love have a unique ability to repair the damaging cardiovascular effects of negative thoughts.

In one interesting study, she created negative feelings in people by showing them disturbing films and having them perform a frustrating task. This caused them to experience cardiovascular distress symptoms, such as higher blood pressure, vascular constriction, and increased heart rate.

Then she tried to return these people to their normal, baseline cardiovascular readings. To do this, she showed some of them funny, happy films, intended to evoke positive feelings. Others were shown films with a neutral content. The rest were not shown any further films, but were given time to recover from their distress.

Only the subjects who'd seen the happy films quickly returned to normal cardiovascular readings. The rest stayed stuck.

In a similar experiment, researchers found that when people experienced positive emotions, it increased their problem-solving ability and mental focus. This, in turn, increased one of the brain's primary contentment neurotransmitters, dopamine.

Thus, positive thoughts not only rescue the body, but also improve

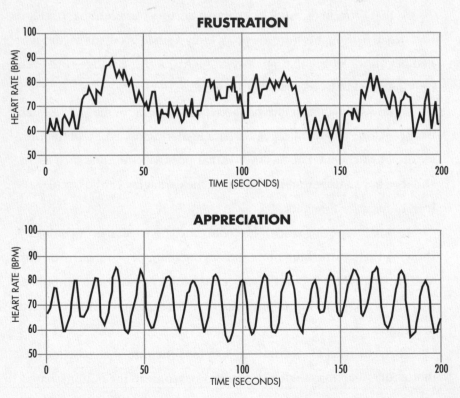

mental function, which then enhances brain biochemistry. Then brain biochemistry inspires positive thoughts, and the whole process begins again. An upward spiral is created! And it's as powerful as the downward spiral of negative thoughts. One kills, the other heals.

Further research also shows that appreciation, in particular, is an unparalleled healing force for mind and body.

The graphs on the opposite page illustrate the tremendous power of appreciation. In this experiment, researchers at the Institute of HeartMath, a California science foundation, monitored heart rhythms, first while people were experiencing frustration, and then while they experienced appreciation. As you can see, during anger the heart rhythm was jerky and random, but during appreciation it was smooth and ordered. The smooth and ordered patterns indicate enhanced nervous system balance and cardiovascular function.

During the same experiment, researchers also monitored the activity of the autonomic nervous system, the involuntary part of the nervous system, which regulates such automatic functions as digestion, immune activity, hormonal output, and blood vessel constriction. The autonomic nervous system is divided into two branches: the sympathetic branch, which tells the body to speed up and be wary, and the parasympathetic branch, which tells the body to slow down and be calm. The sympathetic branch activates the fight-or-flight mechanisms and helps us to survive. The parasympathetic branch activates the rest-and-repair mechanisms, and also the immune system, and helps us to thrive.

Both branches are closely linked to the brain. They are activated by thoughts, which they then reinforce physically. Therefore, they play an important role in the upward spiral of happiness and the downward spiral of fear. The parasympathetic state is especially beneficial to the heart. It creates strong, steady readings in electrocardiograms.

You may be thinking, "That's good, but I'm not worried about my heart, I'm worried about my happiness." But your happiness depends partly upon your heart.

Throughout history, people believed that love comes from the heart, and poets still pay homage to this notion. Surprisingly, the latest science shows that this idea may be based in reality. The function of the heart does affect the mind and emotions, possibly even more than the hormone-producing endocrine system, which is sometimes referred to as the "second brain."

The power of the heart to influence the mind and emotions was first examined scientifically in the early 1990s, mostly in research sponsored by the Institute of HeartMath. Initially, researchers there were intrigued by the fact that transplanted hearts are able to beat immediately upon transplantation, even before nerves coming from the brain are functional.

This occurs, they discovered, because the heart has an intrinsic nervous system of its own, which can cause it to beat even without messages from the brain. This nervous system consists of masses of nerve cells, or neurons, similar to those in the brain. These masses of neurons include parasympathetic and sympathetic neurons that make heartbeat possible: contract, relax, contract, relax. Without them, the heart cannot function. This nervous system has been dubbed the heart-brain.

Most fascinating of all, researchers discovered that the heart-brain even has the power to send messages to the brain. The messages are sent via the spinal cord and through the largest nerve in the body, the vagus nerve, which stretches from the brain to the torso. Therefore, it's outdated to think that nerve messages travel only from head to heart: It's a two-way street.

Because the heart can "speak" to the brain, through the vagus nerve and spinal cord feedback system, it sometimes overrides messages that come from the brain—particularly messages of distress, which can trigger heart attacks.

As researchers continued to study the surprising autonomy of the heart, which was previously considered by most scientists to be just a simple pump, they found that the heart is also an endocrine gland, which secretes its own hormone, ANF (atrial natriuretic factor). ANF influences not only the blood vessels and kidneys, but also the mood-influencing adrenal glands—and the brain.

In the brain, parasympathetic or sympathetic impulses coming from the heart help trigger the onset of either calming or excitatory thoughts. This may be the reason why some heart transplant patients occasionally adopt personality tendencies of their donors, a phenomenon that has been noted since the beginning of heart transplantation.

One recipient, for example, became notably calmer after receiving the heart of an unusually placid person, and another recipient, strange as it seems, reportedly found herself enjoying the favorite foods of her donor, even though she'd never liked them before.

In emotionally healthy people, there appears to be a strong tendency for the heart and brain to have smoothly functioning dialogues, and to remain in synchronization, or entrainment. Entrainment appears not only to reflect a positive frame of mind, but also to help create it, in part by enhancing balance of the autonomic nervous system.

The body, clearly, can help heal the mind. But what inaugurates this healing? The mind itself! Your mind, when focused on appreciation, has an unparalleled power to trigger physical and emotional healing. But it can be hard to focus on appreciation. Too many things get in the way—including fear.

I know a technique, though, that almost always decreases fear. I call it the Appreciation Audit.

The Appreciation Audit helps you bring appreciation to the forefront of your spirit and intellect. When you do this, you have a shield from fear, since fear and appreciation cannot both be processed by the brain at the same time. I created the Appreciation Audit for people who live too much of their lives in fear. Unfortunately, that includes almost all of us.

Doing the Appreciation Audit creates what psychologists call a perceptual shift. This shift doesn't change the facts of your life, but changes how you view them. This new view can help make you happy and give you the power to change.

The Appreciation Audit has several variations, but its basic premise is simply focusing the mind upon appreciation, to the exclusion of everything else—especially negative feelings, such as fear and anger.

To perform the most fundamental form of the Appreciation Audit, reserve 3 to 5 minutes, preferably three times each day, to think about something you deeply appreciate. Many people do it during their commute, since there's not much else to do. It's best to spread it throughout the day, to achieve the maximum physical and psychological effect.

You can focus on anything. It can be your children and the love they bring to your life, or your husband or grandmother. It can be chocolate chip cookies, fishing, your first kiss, or the time you hit a home run. The important thing is the quality of the feeling.

The Appreciation Audit is a form of focused meditation, which has been shown in numerous studies to have a powerful impact upon the balance of the autonomic nervous system, the brain's neurotransmitter profile, the cardiovascular profile, muscular tension, and the psyche. Its effects last long after the exercise has ended, sometimes for several hours. It reprograms the mind and memory by severing the fearful, self-reinforcing thought loops of anxiety that are inaugurated by the amygdala and perpetuated by the neocortex.

Another variation is to concentrate on more than one subject. Some people construct Top Five lists, such as Top Five Favorite People, Top Five All-Time Vacations, Top Five Things I Love about My Son, Top Five Foods, or Top Five Things I'm Looking Forward To.

People often focus their minds on negative things, trying to think them into submission. It's called worry. The Appreciation Audit is the opposite of worry. Because of our cultural obsession with negativity, there has never been a word or phrase for the practice of anti-worry, until now. The closest thing is prayer—but many people focus their prayers on problems.

The Appreciation Audit is great when crises hit. At my urging, a guest with cancer compiled a Top Five list of positive aspects of his disease. It was:

1. My cancer has a good recovery rate.
2. I haven't suffered any permanent effects.
3. I never knew how much my family loved me until now.
4. Because I'm so vigilant now, I'm probably safer than ever.
5. I finally know how much I love life.

He checked his list every time he started to worry, which at first was about 20 times a day. Each time he did it, it broke his negative loop of thoughts, short-circuited his body's fear-reinforcement systems, and lifted his spirits enough for him to see his problem and his challenges realistically instead of pessimistically.

Over time, he stopped playing out worst-case scenarios, a common habit that's called *catastrophizing*. When his catastrophizing stopped, he lost much of his fear of the future, and focused on just the current effects of his cancer, which were insignificant. He realized that fear is *always* of the future, and that he had never been able to control the future before and wouldn't be able to now. His reptile of fear gradually grew weaker, and his spirit began to soar.

Throughout his spiritual growth, I never suggested that he try to see his cancer as a blessing, as devotees of the Woo-Woo School of Psychology might advocate. If cancer is a blessing, I'll take the curse of good health. Appreciating life doesn't mean having to believe that everything happens for the best. I tell people to look for the good in life, not the best. The best doesn't always happen. But good, in one form or another, always does.

And good is good enough. Not even happy people are happy all the time. That's not life. That's not even a good Disney movie.

Life is love: bittersweet, vulnerable, ever-changing, imperfect—and eternally worthy of unbounded appreciation.

Another technique similar to the Appreciation Audit, originated by the HeartMath Institute, is called Freeze Frame. To do it, you concentrate on something you deeply appreciate, but you also focus calming mental energy directly upon your heart. This appears to enhance the rhythm and strength of the heartbeat.

Although heartbeat is involuntary, it can be influenced by conscious thought. Many practitioners of yoga can increase or decrease heartbeat through force of will, and some yoga masters can even slow heartbeat to a barely discernible level, creating a virtual state of suspended animation. Even the average person can warm his or her hands or feet, through increased blood flow, simply by concentrating upon this action.

When calming attention is directed to the heart, heart rhythm slows and intensifies. This helps brain waves, via entrainment, to slow to the calming alpha wave frequency. In the alpha wave condition, it becomes much easier for the mind to focus deeply on positive thoughts.

The Appreciation Audit and Freeze Frame are hard for some people, though, because they're so focused on fear that they've lost touch with what's good in their lives. If it's hard for you to find the love and the other positive feelings that lie dormant in your heart, try a technique that I call Personal Appreciative Inquiry. It's a simple method that helps you find the answers to the major questions of your life: What do I want? What should I do?

Finding the right answers starts with asking the right questions. Asking the wrong questions—such as, Why me?—leads nowhere. Or worse.

Because we live in a survival-obsessed, fearful culture, we're accustomed to asking the wrong questions. We tend to approach every difficult situation with the basic question of, What's wrong? There's a better question: What's right?

Negativity has its place. Asking what's wrong can be effective in an emergency. But even then, it's just half of the equation. Nothing ever gets fixed until someone figures out a positive solution.

Besides, most problems aren't emergencies. They're chronic, complex situations that require rational thought, creativity, and the other emotionally intelligent qualities that fear snuffs out. Fear's sparse repertoire—fighting, fleeing, or freezing—is notoriously ineffective for resolving difficult situations.

The Personal Appreciative Inquiry consists of asking constructive questions that are built for action.

One of my current activities is business consulting, and I adapted the Personal Appreciative Inquiry from a similar business-world process, called Appreciative Inquiry—created by business and organizational consultants David Cooperrider, Ph.D., and Diana Whitney, Ph.D.—that is used by a number of major companies, including GTE and British Airways. Diana Whitney says that Appreciative Inquiry changes a company's approach "from problem-oriented, deficit discourse to possibility-oriented, appreciative discourse."

The Personal Appreciative Inquiry consists of asking constructive questions during these four basic stages of change, identified by Cooperrider and Whitney.

1. **Discovery.** This is the stage in which people identify their own best qualities, which have helped them the most in the past. The questions could range from What am I best at? to What did I do previously that solved a similar situation?

2. **Dream.** This is the stage in which people envision possibilities. The questions could include What's the best thing that could come out of this problem? or Who can help me?

3. **Design.** This is the stage in which people chart a course of action. The

question might be Where's the best place to start? or How long will this take to succeed?

4. **Delivery.** This is the action phase. In this phase, the best questions might be What is the first thing I need to do? What's next? What's the final step?

There are dozens of constructive questions for each stage. But the key element stays the same: Keep questions constructive. This keeps fear from clouding the mind and points the way to solutions. Every question you ask will lead you either to darkness, or to light.

Recently, I had a woman in my office who'd suffered childhood sexual abuse. Other psychologists would probably have asked, "When did the abuse start? How did it make you feel? Do you blame yourself?"

But this old-fashioned approach just doesn't help much. When did it start?—Too early. How did I feel?—Take a guess. Do I blame myself?—No, the rapist.

My first questions were, "When in your life did you cope with this best?" "What were you doing differently then?" I asked her who had given her the most help, and what kind of help had it been. "What friend understands best?" "Did you learn anything good about yourself from the ordeal?"

By the end of the session, she had not resolved her abuse. There is no resolution to an unspeakable experience. As I've said, your worst memories don't go away, and they don't get better.

But *you* can get better. You are more than the sum of your suffering.

This woman got better. But it didn't start by just stirring up her pain. It started when I asked, "How can you get better?" On that subject, she—

not I—was the expert. That's how it always is.

To be happy, you must overcome fear, and the best way to overcome fear is with love. Many people, though, cannot find their love. It exists, but it's buried beneath a cold snowdrift of hate. It's easy to hate. You can hate anything from death to terrorists to an unloving father. But hate does terrible interior damage. It tarnishes love, hides love, and often even kills love.

People often think they can hate some people and love others fully, but it's hard. Love and hate can't live in the same heart. Think of the happiest people you know. They probably don't love just their spouses and kids and hate a number of other people. I'll bet they have a smile for everyone and something good to say about almost anyone. They probably have no enemies—and not much fear.

For the most part, hate is fear. We only hate the things we're afraid of. When someone hurts us terribly, we often hate him for it. But we hate him mostly because we're afraid he'll hurt us again—either literally or in our minds, which replay the scene of hurt again and again. If we had the power to stop him from hurting us ever again—even in our memories— our fear would fade, and our hate would again become just hurt, which can always heal.

We do have a way to stop people from hurting us again and again, even in our memories. It is forgiveness. Forgiveness is the blessing we bestow on not just those who have hurt us, but upon ourselves. Forgiveness knocks down the walls around love that hate can build.

Forgiveness doesn't alter what has happened. The memory remains; the hurt is unchanged. But forgiveness grants us new eyes, through the grace of love, that see the hurt in a different way.

Forgiveness isn't forgetting. It's just leaving behind your own hate and rising to the next level of life. It's not about letting the other guy off the hook—it's about letting yourself off the hook.

From a medical perspective, hate is a heavy burden, creating chronic overstimulation of the sympathetic nervous system, which contributes strongly to depressed immunity, insomnia, hypertension, muscle pain, colitis, ulcers, heart attack, stroke, memory loss, migraines, and impaired cognitive function. But the worst damage is to peace of mind. It's impossible to hate and be happy at the same time.

Many people resist forgiveness because they think it requires a melodramatic outpouring of emotion. But sometimes all you've got to say is something like, "Hi, how's it going? Can I borrow your stepladder?" In psychological healing, melodrama is overrated. It works better in movies than in real life.

You don't even need to tell someone you've forgiven her. You can forgive someone who's dead. The important thing is just to get the hate out of your heart.

For most people, though, the hardest job isn't forgiving others. It's forgiving themselves. The most destructive hate of all is self-hate, and there's an epidemic of it in our self-critical society. This kind of hate usually surfaces as a low-level feeling of self-contempt and self-doubt. People just don't feel good about themselves. When this feeling invades their lives, they always attach a presumed cause to it: I'm too fat, too poor, too lazy . . . the list is endless. But the real cause is almost always the same one that inspires hatred of others: fear. Self-hate is fear of not being loved. When this fear gets a foothold, it always finds a reason to justify its existence. Nobody's perfect, and if you're afraid you're not good enough to be loved, you'll always find an imperfection to feed that fear.

Happy people don't fight the imperfection. They fight the fear. Nobody overcomes this fear easily. The fear of not being enough is strong. But it's not as strong as love.

When you focus your mind and spirit on appreciation of yourself, even this fear fades. But not overnight.

That's why I recommend that people *practice* forgiveness. It *takes* practice.

Some people consider forgiveness to be the highest evolution of appreciation. But research shows that there is one last kind of love that's even greater and even more conducive to happiness: altruism.

Altruism has been called the great paradox: When you give something to someone else, you're the one who feels best. Giving is getting.

Studies show that happy people are altruistic, and that altruistic people are happy. But no researcher has determined which quality comes first. They are that closely connected.

I know you've experienced this. During the holidays, which do you anticipate with greater pleasure—the gifts you'll get, or the gifts you'll give?

Giving is the purest form of appreciation, because it's appreciation in action. It's not a philosophy; it's an experience.

The experience of giving takes you outside yourself and pulls you away from your own problems, fears, and self-involvement. During the act of altruism, you're not worried about your finances, or your health, or anything else.

Some psychologists have asserted—cynically, I believe—that altruism is based on reciprocation: You scratch my back and I'll scratch yours. But that explanation overlooks the obvious: Doing something good *feels* good, in and of itself. It awakens your love and bonds you with other people. When this bond is formed, it not only gives you a better feeling about the person you're helping, but about all people in general. Whatever mistrust you may have had about the human race is diminished. You feel less fear.

As love increases, fear decreases. Even your love for yourself increases. This is partly because you feel greater self-esteem, and partly because you have more love to go around.

In an experiment on altruism at the Harvard Medical School, researchers showed people a documentary of Mother Teresa that was intended to evoke feelings of altruism. Researchers then measured a component of the subjects' immune systems (immunoglobulin-A), which is decreased by anxiety. The levels had increased. Thus, altruism overcomes fear.

Because altruism is the purest form of appreciation, it empowers you to love people even when they don't love you. When I was young, I once complained to my mom that a woman I was head over heels in love with didn't feel as strongly about me. I've always remembered what she said. She told me that no two people ever love each other the same—and that whoever loves the most is the lucky one.

In the final analysis, you can't really feel someone else loving you. That love is *their* experience, not yours. You can only feel it when you love them. That feeling is yours. It's the best feeling in the world, and it's the one feeling that can always defeat your fear and make you happy.

Not long ago, I got a phone call from one of my clients, a distraught woman who lives in a Manhattan skyscraper. She told me that when she looked out of one of her windows, she could see all the way up to Central Park, glistening with green, and that it was beautiful and full of peace. But when she looked out another window, she saw the ugly rubble of the World Trade Center. She didn't know how to handle it.

I could have told her, "Well, look at the park."

But I told her to look into the rubble. Don't be afraid to look at it, I told her, and don't be afraid to see the broken hearts, and the pain, and the insane waste. It's there, and there's no denying it. But there was more to see in that rubble than just pain. There was also courage, and great compassion.

I told her she should try to feel what the firemen must have felt as they rushed into those teetering buildings. They had to have been feeling fear. Had to. But still they rushed in, one after another, shoulder to shoulder, by the hundreds—because even more than they felt fear, they must have felt love. For strangers. Total strangers.

And here's the true miracle of it: This was not unusual.

This happens somewhere, on a smaller scale, every day. It happens to firefighters, police officers, rescue workers, and soldiers—and even to people like you.

Every day, you go places you fear—in your memories, in your thoughts of the future, and in your real life. Through the grace of God, the fears you face are almost always less horrifying than running into a burning building. But your fears are no less real to you, and are sometimes just as frightening. There may have been times you sat by a phone, waiting for a biopsy result. You may have sat in an airplane that was lurching in a lightning storm, wondering if you'd feel the ground again. Maybe you've wondered how you were going to feed your family with no job. Maybe you've paced a hospital waiting room, as I once did, praying that someone you love will still be there to love tomorrow.

Your prayers are not always answered—not the way you'd like. Tragedy is a given. We are all mortal, and are all made vulnerable by love.

But we are made strong by love, too. If we so choose.

Tomorrow is the first Saturday of my life without my father. I am going to go hunting, but with no hope of him being there, as he has been so many times before. I miss my dad with all my heart, and I am afraid to go.

I could cancel it. That would be so easy right now. I could let my bleeding wound heal.

But I *know* that I am going to have a good weekend. I'm certain of it. I'll wake up late and have a big breakfast with my wife in the shining September sun. Then I'm going to go to the football game.

And then I am going to go hunting, with the spirit of my father, in the mountains we both love.

Life is so beautiful.

CHAPTER FIVE

Hearing the Voice of the Heart

I opened a door. And my life changed forever. Bramm! Bramm! Bramm! Rifle shots! That's what it sounded like, and I inadvertently ducked. Bramm! The vibration traveled right through me.

But there in a corner was a young woman named Kate, and it wasn't a gun that was making that violent explosion, but her own head, capped in a helmet, as she battered it into a hard plaster wall.

Just moments before—this was back in 1973—I had been striding down the halls of the Nebraska Psychiatric Institute as a newly minted psychology intern, confident that I could treat any of the mental maladies from my textbooks that I had memorized.

But, Kate! My God—she bore such little resemblance to . . . a case history.

Appalled at the violence she was doing to herself, I turned to the nurse who had led me here. "Isn't someone going to help her?" I asked.

"Yes. Soon."

"Who?"

"You."

"*How?*"

"Don't ask me," she said in a tired tone. "Poor Kate's hopeless. Impossible."

I was scared out of my mind. The door closed. Bramm! Bramm! Bramm! I sat there. I had just gotten my warm welcome to the world of cynical psychology.

The first thing I realized was that nothing I had learned in academia was going to help Kate. If the conventional approaches had been capable of helping her, they already would have. Kate had previously been treated by several teams of prominent doctors, with almost 25 different modalities. She had been sprayed with ammonia when she'd banged her head, and one doctor had wanted to shock her with a device resembling a cattle prod. They had tried to talk Kate out of banging her head, but that hadn't worked because she was developmentally disabled, with a very low I.Q. They had tried to reward her with candy for not doing it. No dice. One doctor had theorized that her head banging was an idiosyncratic symptom of epilepsy, but antiseizure medication hadn't helped. Nor had powerful tranquilizers.

She was not autistic. She was not schizophrenic. She did not have any classic form of psychosis.

One Freudian theorist had said that Kate was banging her head in order to mask the pain of a conflicted psyche, but guess how much good that did.

Eventually, the doctors did come up with what's called a dual diagnosis: anxiety disorder characterized by compulsive tendencies, plus developmental disability. It didn't help Kate, but it sure made the doctors feel better.

Bramm! Bramm! The rhythm of the banging was hypnotic and horrible, like the crack of a whip on someone's back. When you see someone inflicting that kind of self-punishment, your instinct is to recoil in disgust, and that's what most of the people at the institute had done, leaving Kate in her own desolate isolation. But I couldn't just fill out her chart and leave. It wasn't in me.

Bramm! Bramm! And then . . . nothing. The silence was sweet, an oasis. I took the opportunity to look into Kate's eyes. She stared back with no emotion, no recognition. Her eyes were empty. All I could see in them was a reflection of myself.

"Where are you, Kate?" I asked softly. "Are you in there?"

I thought she was. But where?

Here's what I know now: Kate was in the same place that everyone is who has lost the feeling that they can choose the direction of their own life: trapped in depression and helplessness, with no sense of self.

She appeared to have no appreciation at all for life—understandable, in her circumstances—and that helped to lock her in her fearful lower-brain functions. Her reptile was ruling.

Even so, the silence. It had been several minutes now.

Then it dawned on me—a concept so obvious it was virtually invisible: She could stop her head banging.

She did have the personal power to quit destroying herself. She just didn't know it. Nor, apparently, did anyone else.

At that moment, I knew that the cure was in her, not in me. My only job was to get her to see that she had the power and had the choice.

I took her hand. Held it gently. After some time, slowly, mechanically, she turned toward me. She raised her eyes.

They say the eyes are the windows to the soul, and for at least those few seconds, that was true. There she was! Not so different. Just alone and powerless—impotent, helpless. Unhappy.

I wondered how long it had been since someone had held her hand.

I sat there feeling helpless myself. I was supposed to be the ward's hot, new shrink—Young Dr. Freud—but I felt like nothing more than Young Dr. Handholder.

I knew, based on what I'd already seen, that neither reward nor restraint could stop her. The only way to keep Kate from banging her head would be to make her choose not to. But how do you *make* someone choose? If you do, it's not choice.

Choice is the voice of the heart. It's honesty in action. That's why it's so powerful.

Even in my befuddlement, though, I managed to see the obvious: When I held Kate's hand, she seemed to feel better. She was appreciably calmer, and the desolate look in her eyes softened. Already, I'd learned a lesson: The isolation of fear can be overcome—often quickly, without years of psychotherapy. And when it is, possibilities can begin to form, even for people whose circumstances seem totally devoid of them.

At this point, though, I wasn't really trying to bring happiness or fulfillment to Kate's life. That was too much to hope for. I just wanted to bring *life* to Kate's life.

Later that day, I mentioned Kate to the crusty old head of the pediatrics unit, and I remember him saying, "Oh, that one. Her options are extremely limited." As in nonexistent. I didn't buy it. Where I came from—the "can-do" rural Midwest, in the 1960s era of limitless horizons—*everyone* had possibilities. Even people like Kate.

Possibilities, I still believe, exist for all of us, even for those of us who are blessed the least—even for those of us (and maybe this is you) who are backed into a corner.

Possibilities, in fact, are not only ever-present, but indispensable. They are as necessary for the life of the mind as oxygen is for the life of the body.

The false perception of having no possibilities feels like jail. It creates a sensation of helplessness that is deadly to the mind and spirit. This helplessness leads to depression and anxiety, and often creates anger, obsessiveness, self-destructiveness, hopelessness, and a sense of victimization. I see people with this problem every day.

But possibilities, once they are recognized, help wipe out these deadly feelings and offer us the chance to choose. And it is choice, ultimately, that creates our identities. Choice, and only choice, is what makes each person unique.

Even though possibilities always exist, we lose sight of them when we are blinded by fear. This fear usually starts when we fail once too often, or when we are thwarted too many times by the people around us. When this happens, our problem-solving creativity shrivels. At worst, it narrows to just fighting, fleeing, and freezing. We become merely reactive, instead of proactive. Problems become prisons.

Freedom from these self-imposed prisons comes only when we suspend fear by evoking appreciation, envisioning all of our remaining possibilities, and then choosing one.

Choice is proactivity, and choice is power. It charts the course of our lives. It makes us happy.

The next time I saw Kate, the first thing I did was reach out to her and make a connection. As Kate began to calm, her head banging slowed, and again, it momentarily stopped. When that happened, I said to her softly, "Kate, let's forget about why you bang your head. Let's focus on what you're doing when you're *not* banging your head."

Later on, I would call this the 60-Minute Principle: focusing on the few minutes in every hour when someone is functioning well, instead of focusing only on her failures. The goal is to stretch out the good minutes until they take up the entire hour. Back then, though, I wasn't trying to invent a new approach. I was just working with what I had.

Looking at the sterile room around us—this compassionately constructed cage—I felt a powerful urge to get out, and I couldn't help but think Kate would want out, too. I opened the door, and we walked down the hall. I had to escort her down the middle of it to prevent her from banging her head against its walls. Even so, she banged her head on my shoulder. Thunk! Thunk! Thunk!

I opened the institute's big front doors. Suddenly we were enveloped by a lovely, spring-soft morning, green and yellow with trees and sun. A warm breeze riffled over us, and Kate startled. I felt her hand tighten and then relax. How long had it been since she'd been outdoors?

Her head seemed to rise out of her shoulders. Over the next several minutes, her eyes lost some of their inward focus and reached out to the richly beautiful world we all inhabit. With the smell of flowers heavy in the air, Kate seemed—for those few moments—overwhelmed with appreciation for the world. A butterfly fluttered by, a yellow and black tiger swallowtail, and Kate tracked it with her eyes as it lit on a flower beside us. She seemed mesmerized, and not at all inclined to butt her head. Who, after all, has ever tried to bang her head against a butterfly?

I wanted Kate to take her life back from all the well-meaning people who'd stolen it from her. My goal was to awaken her sense of appreciation, and then get her to start making choices, so she'd feel like a person instead of a . . . case.

I started with a simple exercise, just telling her that I was going to go outside and that she could come if she wanted. At first, she'd just sit on her bed ignoring me, rhythmically rocking. I would open the door and stand out in the hallway for as long as an hour, periodically asking her if she wanted to come. It was like trying to coax a toddler into taking medicine.

Finally, Kate would get up, and we'd walk outside together.

I did a dozen variations of this. Outdoors, when the path forked, I would wait until she chose which way to go. In the beginning, it was a paralyzing decision. I also had her choose between two candies, and choose which of three caps to wear. Every day, I introduced her to new possibilities and new choices.

As I did it, I became aware of how many choices there really are in each day, and of how often most people just sleepwalk through the day on automatic pilot, doing what they've always done instead of choosing what they really want.

It took time, believe me, but gradually Kate began to come alive.

The more choices she made, the more she came out of her shell and stopped banging her head. The number of minutes in every hour in which she hurt herself began to dwindle. It confirmed my belief that her healthy minutes were the key to her recovery, even though all the other doctors were still preoccupied with her dysfunction.

I soon saw that there was one time when she rarely banged her head: anytime she had something better to do. If there was something fun in her immediate environment, she'd choose it. But I couldn't make her do it. You can't force fun.

Gradually, she began to fulfill more of her own needs. The hospital staff, I realized with sadness, had almost destroyed her natural desire to take care of herself.

As she progressed, I announced an ambitious plan. I wanted Kate to support herself.

Support herself? Kate? My God!—I thought they were going to lock *me* up. But I was serious.

I began to teach her a complex, 28-step procedure for assembling bicycle brakes. It was a paying job that she could do in a sheltered workshop. The bike brakes were heavy enough to have some heft to them, and this helped her to learn kinesthetically, which relies less on upper-brain function. It was hard on both of us—two steps forward and one step back every day—but there was never a day she chose not to do it.

Increasingly, she began to reach for the brake and demand, "I do it by self." Soon, it was just the shorthand, "Self!"

And, indeed, a "self" was being formed.

I remember the day she mastered the last step. She locked the brake into place with a final, confident *clank!*—and looked up at me with wonder and joy.

She held it out to me, as a gift.

"Self!" she proclaimed. It brought tears to my eyes.

We walked up and down every corridor of that hospital, showing every doctor and nurse we could find what she had done. Some of them were slack-jawed with amazement. A few—those who'd shown the least interest in her—seemed ashamed, almost reluctant to believe it.

But *she* reached out to *them*. Kate had learned more than just building brakes.

The last time I ever saw Kate, she was living in a pleasant, community assisted-care home, with good friends, a nice room, and a steady income. As I arrived, she was rushing out the door to go bowling with her friends, and she looked so happy, just ecstatic. In the commotion, I didn't think she'd recognize me.

But she spotted me. Ran over. Threw her arms around me. Wouldn't let go.

That was the best pay I ever got, that hug. The happiness that came from that hug lasted a long time.

And it made me embrace forever a universal truth: Everyone has possibilities. *Everyone*. And choosing among them is the feast of our human existence.

At about this same time, I was beginning to notice journal articles by a maverick young psychologist named Dr. Martin Seligman. The articles were riveting, revolutionary.

Dr. Seligman was leaving behind the safe landscape of clinical psychology's disease/treatment model and was heading . . . who knew where? He seemed to be aimed toward the horizon of a new psychology, where disease was not the sole definition of the human psyche. But if disease wasn't, what was?

These days, Dr. Seligman is one of the most respected voices in the field of psychology, and is a past president of the American Psychological Association. He is regarded as the father of positive psychology and has been called "the Freud of the 21st century" by *Newsweek* magazine.

Back then, though, amid no small controversy, he was shocking the world of psychology by focusing on what makes people mentally healthy, instead of what makes them mentally ill. And his first groundbreaking, earthshaking work dealt with choice.

Dr. Seligman believed that having options and making choices is the very foundation of human psychological health. Life can be brutal, he said, but if we always have options, we'll always have hope. And hope, or optimism, he believed, was our greatest blessing—the one thing we still can have when everything else is gone.

However, when we feel as if we've exhausted all our possibilities and are left with no viable choices, then our suffering really starts. This condition, he demonstrated, is the worst single poison to the human psyche. It creates depression, anxiety, and apathy. It destroys the body, mind, and spirit. It kills us even while we still walk the earth.

But choice can be reinstated, he said, and when it is, it is a veritable elixir for human happiness.

Learning to Be Unhappy

In one of the most important psychological experiments of the last 100 years, young university professor Martin Seligman placed dogs, one at a time, in sealed boxes, from which there was no escape. He placed other dogs in open boxes that did allow escape. Then both sets of dogs were subjected to mild electrical shocks from the floors of their boxes. The dogs in the open boxes quickly learned to jump out. The dogs that had no possibility of escape, however, soon gave up trying to get away from the shocks and laid down, passively accepting their fates. They had learned to feel helpless.

The same dogs were then individually placed in two-compartment boxes, with one side safe from shock. The dogs that had previously been in the open boxes quickly learned to escape the shocks by going to the safe compartments. However, most of the dogs that had already learned to feel helpless stayed in the compartments that shocked them, whining with misery but passively accepting their pain.

These famous experiments were later replicated by other researchers, proving that learned helplessness is a common phenomenon that often dominates the attitudes of not only animals, but also people. And when it does dominate, it causes untold damage. It creates a nearly constant state of psychological stress, characterized by depression and anxiety, that I sometimes call 24-hour-a-day guard duty.

This state strikes when people feel powerless to manage their own environments, and thus ensure their own survival. It brings the fears of not having enough and not being enough roiling to the surface. These fears become so overwhelming that many people don't even try to fight back or flee—they just freeze, and passively wait for the threats to go away.

As this state of mental stress festers, it feeds into physical stress. It overactivates the stimulating sympathetic nervous system, which then triggers release of stress hormones, including cortisol. These physical stressors deplete immunity, hurt the heart, and contribute to numerous illnesses.

Worst of all, the physical reactions reinforce the mental malaise by depleting the contentment neurotransmitters serotonin and dopamine.

This depletion was proved when researchers gave animals with

What Happy People Know

learned helplessness various drugs, including opioids and antidepressants, that increased their feel-good neurotransmitters. When they did this, most of the animals stopped their passive, helpless behavior. However, when they gave them the opposite types of drugs—those that, like psychological stress, inhibit contentment neurotransmitters—the animals' helplessness returned.

Thus, because the stress of learned helplessness can invade even our brain biochemistries, it can perpetuate an endless cycle of negative thoughts. When this cycle of helplessness takes over the mind, it contributes to three primary errors of perception. It creates:

1. **Permanence**—thinking that a problem will last forever
2. **Personalization**—thinking that every problem is your fault
3. **Pervasiveness**—thinking that one problem extends to every other situation

When people become mired in this quicksand of misperception, it blights their entire outlook on life.

Learned helplessness can overtake almost anyone, but it most often occurs in three basic situations: when someone fails too many times, when someone is boxed in by a double-bind, lose-lose situation, or when someone is dominated by somebody else who takes away his opportunity to choose.

But each of these three common causes of learned helplessness can be overcome. If repeated failure is making you feel helpless, remember that failure occurs only when you quit. Thomas Edison failed to invent the lightbulb the first 2,000 times he tried.

If you feel as if you're boxed into a hopeless, double-bind situation, make a strong effort to look outside the box for an innovative solution. And remember that no double-bind situation ruins the entirety of life or lasts forever.

Most important of all, be brave enough to resist when someone else wants to steal your right to make your own decisions. If you follow the voice of your heart, you'll probably make the right decision. And even if you're wrong, you'll learn something. Tom Watson, the founder of IBM, made a fortune by letting his managers make their own decisions. Once, when one of those decisions was wrong, causing a $10 million loss, the manager offered to resign. But Watson replied, "What? After I just spent 10 million dollars on your education?"

Most people who want to rob others of their right to make choices do it because they feel powerless themselves. Insecurity is a typical trait of a tyrant.

But there is a force far stronger than insecurity that also often makes people steal your choices. You must be careful of this force. It's love.

Love, at its best, gives meaning to our lives. But love can also victimize.

A Victim of Love

"Who's going to love me now?" sobbed Vic, as he looked down at his paralyzed and shrinking body. "Who's going to love . . . *this*?"

What could I say? Vic's dilemma was gut-wrenching. Only a month earlier, he'd been a ladies' man and a linebacker, with his life unfolding like a flower. And then his dad had talked him into taking a ride on a motorcycle, a truck had pulled out in front of them, and his dad had dumped the bike. Vic's head had smashed into the curb. Vic had ended up in the pediatrics ward of the University of Nebraska Hospital, where I was working. He had become a hemiplegic, with the entire right side of his body inert and numb.

Every day his dad came to the hospital and stayed until late at night, when hospitals develop an unnatural quiet, punctuated only by distant echoes in faraway rooms that remind you of the vastness of suffering. Sometimes in this quiet, I could hear Vic's dad crying as he sat by his sleeping son. It was a terrible sound, one of those things you try to forget, but can't.

By the next morning, though, Vic's dad would have his happy face on, and would start doing all the jobs that he hadn't done for his son since Vic had been an infant: bathing him, cutting his food, helping him go to the bathroom, dressing him.

But dad was doing too much, and it was reinforcing Vic's helplessness.

After a couple of weeks, I suggested to Vic's dad that he take a break and do something for himself. "I can't do that," he said, his face drooping with grief. "Not after what I . . ." He couldn't continue. I've never seen such guilt. He hurried back to his son's side, to help Vic get dressed for a meeting with an ex-girlfriend.

Vic couldn't decide what to wear. His indecision struck me. When he'd first entered the hospital, despite his rage and shock, he'd known what he'd wanted and had called his own shots. But his will seemed to be atrophying along with his muscles.

After the former girlfriend left, Vic's dad came in and fussed over him some more, until Vic finally lost his patience and yelled at him. Even so, Vic didn't want his dad to go home. The echoes in the hospital's night-quiet scared him. They seemed like an omen of his empty life ahead.

Dad sat in the hallway for the rest of the night.

Soon after that, the head of physical rehab took me aside and insisted that dad stop waiting on Vic. Vic had a precious window of opportunity in which his brain could still transfer functions to its undamaged areas. This was a use-it-or-lose-it time, and Vic was losing it. (Later on, I learned that in the realm of choice, it's always use-it-or-lose-it time.)

I scheduled a meeting with the father and told him the biggest challenge of his life was just ahead. You've got to love Vic in a way that allows him to be himself, I said.

As I look back, I can see that it was appreciation for Vic that I was asking for. Love—and I mean true love, real love—can cripple us. It can make us miserable, and even dangerous to those we love. It can make us jealous, clingy, overprotective, guilt-ridden, and even vengeful. But appreciation is pure. It's the kind of love that can let us step away, and even watch a loved one suffer, when suffering is what they need.

"If you don't cut the apron strings," I told Vic's dad, "you're going to lose him in a way you haven't even thought about."

"What way?"

"You're going to castrate him," I said bluntly.

He started in again about how guilty he felt, but I cut him off. "You feel guilty because you think you weren't good enough as a dad. But you weren't a bad dad. You were just one hell of an unlucky dad." I put my hands on his shoulders. I had been an unlucky dad myself. "Luck happens," I said softly—or words to that effect.

I told him, as gently as I could, that he was as paralyzed emotionally as his son was physically, and that surrendering his own life and giving up on his own choices wasn't helping anybody. It was just making Vic into an invalid. And him, too. I reminded him that self-sacrifice is usually just selfishness disguised as generosity. There's almost always a hidden agenda in it somewhere (his was getting rid of his guilt).

"What do *you* feel like doing now?" I asked.

He must have sat there for 5 minutes. "Going to a movie," he said finally, in a faraway voice.

"Go."

When he got back, he seemed lighter and looser, and his mood rubbed off onto Vic. He told Vic all about the movie, and they made a plan to see it together the first day Vic got out. As the hospital's quiet began to descend, Vic asked his dad for some help with something, but his dad gently refused. "You've gotta learn to do all that stuff yourself, Vic. So you can get the hell out of here."

Vic smiled a little. For the first time, I think he was picturing himself leaving. Or maybe he just loved his dad for the vote of confidence.

Vic reached out. They embraced. It was an embrace of true equals, of brave men.

For Vic, that was the beginning. He was young and strong, and he fought hard to get his body back. Function returned slowly, but it returned. He wasn't the same as he had been, of course. None of us are ever the same after life and luck get done with us. We change—for better or for worse. Depending upon what we choose.

Vic changed for the better. He became wiser, deeper. Early on, when I had first met him, he'd grimly told me that the accident had been his "destiny." Later, after he'd gone back to school and found a new girlfriend—and found happiness—he told me that he didn't believe in destiny anymore. We remake our destiny every day, he said, by what we do—and what we don't.

I think Vic was right. I don't believe in destiny anymore, either. I believe in choice.

I believe in choice because you can't get to happiness without it.

It took me a long time to figure that out. When I was young, I believed the same nonsense that a lot of people believe about happiness—that it comes from the flashy veneer of the American dream: money, status, and power. But then I grew up (unlike too many other people, who only grow older) and I began to see that these things often destroyed happiness. I learned that happiness only comes from inner qualities, such as courage, altruism, and optimism.

Happiness comes from the self. But where is the self? *Who* is the self? Who are *you*?

If you don't know, you'll never be happy, because you'll never be able to connect with the inner, core qualities that make happiness possible. You'll just travel through life in circles, always going, always intent—never arriving, never content.

You should, in fact, be able to describe exactly who you are, right now, in the proverbial 25 words or less.

Here, for example, is who I am: I'm a family man who loves the outdoors and is working on an exciting new approach to psychology. Why am I so sure that that's who I am? Because that's exactly whom I chose to be. I put tremendous effort into making those choices. I eliminated many other possibilities and poured my heart into the ones that fit me best.

As I made those choices, I also discovered something that now seems obvious, but which seems to escape many people: Choosing *feels* good. Like all the happiness tools, it is intrinsically satisfying. There's nothing like the feeling of calling the shots in your own life. It's better than struggling to make people like you by always doing what they choose. It's better than the career success you can achieve by doing what you're told. It's better than the security of the beaten path.

According to happiness research, choosing feels better than almost anything.

This was shown recently by researcher Kennon Sheldon, Ph.D., of the University of Missouri. Dr. Sheldon conducted three large studies aimed at finding out what brings people the greatest satisfaction. Two of his studies involved American college students, and one involved students from South Korea, to determine if cultural differences changed what makes people feel good.

Dr. Sheldon's studies tested the validity of self-determination theory, a concept that says people are happiest when they're able to make their own choices. The subjects in the studies were asked to recall their most satisfying recent events, and to describe what made the events feel so good.

The results were a stunning confirmation of self-determination theory. The main thing that made the events feel good was the sense of being in charge of them.

This sense of being in charge included experiencing feelings of autonomy, competence, and self-esteem. These feelings finished in three out of the top four positions, among 11 feelings that made people feel good. Bringing up the rear were having money, being popular, and having power (or influence) over others.

Here's the complete list of what makes events satisfying.

1. Autonomy; self-esteem; relatedness (three-way tie)
2. Competence

3. Pleasure

4. Self-actualization; physical thriving (tie)

5. Security

6. Popularity; influence (tie)

7. Money

Dr. Sheldon also did a similar study showing that the feeling of autonomy is priceless for reaching goals. His premise was that "not all personal goals are personal." Some goals, he said, are foisted off on us by other people.

In this study, he examined the goal of doing well during the first year of college. An old aphorism says that there are only two reasons a person goes to college: (1) because your parents did, or (2) because your parents didn't. The implication is that the choice always comes more from your parents than you. However, there's surely a third reason why some people go: because *they* choose to.

Dr. Sheldon sorted out a large group of incoming freshmen according to the source of their goals. He divided them into two basic groups—those who had created their own college goals and those who hadn't. He found that those who had created their own goals were much more likely to achieve them.

He also found that this initial success could be a springboard for continued achievement, if students kept reaching their goals. When goals come from the heart, he said, "Success begets further success," and creates "a spiral of success."

Another important reason choice feels good is because it is the ultimate expression of free will. Free will defines us as human beings and is the foundation of self-esteem. We only have self-esteem when we act in accord with our own values, and to do this, we've got to make choices—oftentimes tough ones. It's not easy to live up to your values. But when you choose to follow your beliefs, you get a feeling like no other.

Every major religion exalts the free-will exercise of choice. In the Judeo-Christian tradition, it's the exercise of choice between good and evil—as expressed in the Garden of Eden story—that defines mankind as special on this earth. When Adam and Eve ate the fruit from the Tree of Knowledge of Good and Evil, they became fully human. From then on, their descendants were forever faced with a constant series of choices between good and evil. These choices separate us from the rest of the animal kingdom, which is driven primarily by instinct rather than spirit and intellect. When we embrace choice, the reptile no longer rules.

Thus, choice is the human burden—and the human blessing. It is our only path to genuine appreciation of self, and this aspect of appreciation is absolutely indispensable for happiness. If you don't love yourself, you can't possibly love your life.

Every choice has consequences, and these consequences create our lives—for better or for worse.

Furthermore, when taken to its extreme, the act of making important life choices can be far more than just satisfying. It can literally be enlightening. This occurs when someone achieves a moment of ultimate understanding of his or her heart, soul, and self. This moment is so electrifying that it is generally described with a religious term: epiphany.

For thousands of years, people have known that epiphanies occasionally occur. Contrary to myth, though, they rarely seem to occur spontaneously, or to people who are ignorant of their own inner lives.

They generally occur to people with strong spiritual inclinations, during episodes of intense inward focus, such as prayer, meditation, or introspection. A meta-analysis of studies over the past 40 years indicates that approximately 30 percent to 40 percent of all Americans have experienced, at least once, a "powerful, spiritual force" that changed their perspective on life.

In just the past decade, researchers have been able to monitor what happens in the brain during these moments, using advanced imaging techniques. They've discovered that during experiences of epiphany, the amygdala, the brain's warehouse of fear, becomes temporarily inactive. There is also a decline in activity in the temporal lobes, which create consciousness about time, and in the parietal lobes, which govern orientation in space (and create the division between self and others). At the same time, activity is heightened in the prefrontal cortex, the primary functional site of the spirit and intellect. Especially active is the left side of the prefrontal cortex, which generates positive feelings and soothes negative feelings.

Interestingly, these are the same basic activities that have been noted to occur in the brain when subjects consciously suspend fear, by engaging in appreciation, and then begin to envision various possibilities for problem solving.

Thus, there is an almost mystical power in the relatively simple act of suspending worry and engaging in choice. When this is done with passion, it can be a genuine spiritual experience. It can connect you to your inner self and attune you to the voice of your heart.

The act of choice is so powerful that it even has dominion over an aspect of our lives that we generally see as beyond our control: perception.

What Happy People Know

People generally think that they simply perceive things the way they are, and have no choice over it.

Not true.

The Life-Changing Quarter-Second

You can change the way you perceive things. Nothing is set in stone—not even the way you're perceiving the world around you at this moment.

In every moment of life and every instance of perception, there is a point of opportunity in which you can choose how you perceive the world.

This ability to alter perception is one of your greatest human abilities. It means that no matter how difficult your life may become, you will always have the power to rise above suffering. It means that you can choose a perspective on reality that will enrich you instead of diminish you.

Many people, however, don't use this power. Some don't even know it exists. They're leaves in the wind, helplessly hoping that fate will be kind. These passive people are just reactive, instead of proactive, and it often ruins their lives. In particular, they're reactive to fear.

It's easy to be that way, since the brain is hardwired for fear. One "wire" in your fear circuitry that can be especially destructive is the tiny neural thread, consisting of just a single elongated brain cell, that runs straight from your primary area of perception to your fear warehouse, your amygdala. This primary area of perception is called the thalamus; it's the part of your brain that receives all of the messages from your eyes, ears, and other sensory organs. The thalamus is your brain's window to the world.

When your thalamus gets messages, it relays them to two places. One is the amygdala. The other is the prefrontal neocortex, the primary functional site of your intellect and spirit.

The amygdala gets the messages from the thalamus first, since it has the advantage of its one-neuron express lane running straight from the thalamus. This speed is great for the survival process. Almost instantly, your amygdala lets you know if you need to respond with fighting, fleeing, or freezing.

Your neocortex is much further from your perception center, though, so it gets the messages much more slowly. But when it does get them, it has wondrous powers of evaluation. It's not a one-note symphony, like the amygdala, which registers mostly just pure fear. When the neocortex gets its messages, it doesn't launch a knee-jerk reaction, as the amygdala does, but stops to consider them. During this consideration, it consults the amygdala, in an ongoing dialogue, but it isn't overly influenced by the amygdala's predictable fearfulness.

The good news is, most of your sensory input is shipped by the thalamus to the neocortex, instead of to the amygdala. The neocortex gets about 95 percent of your incoming messages, while only about 5 percent go straight to your amygdala.

But that 5 percent can wreak havoc! It can set off an illogical chain reaction of fear that's hard to stop. This chain reaction can include igniting the action portion of your fear system—the endocrine glands and the heart's intrinsic nervous system. This makes your heart pump fast and your muscles grow tight. It gets you ready for a fight.

Unfortunately, when these physical responses are added to negative thoughts, fear can gain an irresistible momentum. As the early psychologist William James noted, "Panic is increased by flight, and giving way to the symptoms of anger increases those passions themselves."

The panic that is created by the amygdala feeds upon itself and obliterates reason. Negative thoughts begin to come out of nowhere and overwhelm the neocortex. Fear begins to develop a life of its own. The brain, in effect, gets hijacked by fear.

But here is the saving grace of the situation: There is a moment—lasting approximately one-quarter of a second—when this hijacking can be prevented.

This quarter-second, first reported by the influential psychotherapist and author Tara Bennett-Goleman in *Emotional Alchemy*, was discovered by neurosurgeon Benjamin Libet. A number of years ago, Dr. Libet became interested in the possible existence of a lag time between when people get the urge to take action and when they actually take it. Therefore, he conducted a fascinating neurological experiment on patients undergoing certain brain surgeries, who were awake and alert. He asked them to move one of their fingers, while he electronically monitored their brain activity. That's when he found it—the life-changing quarter-second! There was a quarter-second delay, he discovered, between the urge to move the finger, and its actual movement.

This means that every urge you will ever have—including every fearful urge and every angry urge—contains a quarter-second window of opportunity in which you can disengage from that urge.

The significance of this is extraordinary.

One-quarter of a second may not sound like much time, but in the arena of thought, it's a virtual eternity. It's more than enough time for you to choose to interpret perceptions differently.

This quarter-second is your ultimate power over perception.

It's enough time to realize that a loud noise isn't a bomb, that a stick in the grass isn't a snake, that a sarcastic remark wasn't intended to hurt you, or that slipping on a banana peel is funny instead of irritating.

Taking advantage of this quarter-second is somewhat similar to counting to 10 before allowing yourself to become angry. If you've done this, you've probably realized that you had more control than you'd thought. But it doesn't take 10 seconds to assert this control. It only takes a fraction of a second.

In every moment of life, we have the option of being automatically reactive—and limiting our options to just fighting, fleeing, or freezing—or using the life-changing quarter-second to engage in choice and expand our options.

If you constantly forsake this quarter-second, though, and stay on the automatic pilot of reactivity, you can become enslaved by your fear and anger. When the amygdala is allowed to repeatedly hijack the brain, it grows more adept at doing so, and becomes what some neurologists call a hot amygdala: overly reactive, too sensitive. This happens because our pathways of connected brain cells are, in a way, similar to paths in a forest: The more the paths are used, the easier they are to travel.

A hot amygdala can make a person become what's called a hot reactor, someone who flies off the handle into fits of anger, depression, or anxiety. These people lose all power over their perceptions. After their outbursts, they're likely to say things such as "I don't know what got into me," or "Something in me just snapped." Usually, they see their flights of fear and aggression as separate from their real selves. They'll say things like "That was just my anger talking, not me." Or "I didn't really mean it."

They're right about one thing—their hyperemotional outbursts didn't come from their real selves. Their real selves, centered in their spirits and intellects, probably abhorred the outbursts as much as everyone else.

These outbursts aren't necessary. The intellect and spirit can prevent them, if given the opportunity. A sterling example of this kind of mental and spiritual power came from the great Victor Frankl, the psychiatrist who survived a Nazi death camp. In the camp, Frankl found that he had absolutely no control—except for control over the one aspect of his life that mattered most: his own perceptions. He became exquisitely capable of seeing past anger, despair, hate, and fear, focusing instead on the life-affirming feelings that lie beneath the surface of every situation.

When others saw only humiliation, Frankl saw the humility that made the humiliation bearable. When others saw only despair, Frankl saw the battered hope that underlies all despair and separates it from res-ignation. When others saw only the horror of victims struggling to sur-vive, Frankl saw the courage of victims struggling to survive.

Once, in the ugliness of the camp, Frankl found a flower growing in mud, and saw only the flower, and not the filth that nourished it.

Victor Frankl emerged from this living hell as a better man. And even a happier man.

The power to choose perception is really that strong.

I saw another fine example of this power just yesterday. I was talking to a happy man—but one who had little obvious reason to feel happy. He is an extremely successful businessman. Or was. This year, his high-tech company disintegrated in value from a worth of hundreds of mil-lions to just a few pennies on the dollar. He, personally, lost approximately $75 million—almost all of what he'd spent a lifetime earning.

I asked him how it felt to lose so much. The moment I said it, his whole face tightened, and I thought he was on the edge of an outburst. But he caught himself—the magic quarter-second!—took a breath, and released it as a deep, rolling belly-laugh. "I never thought I'd be in the position to lose 75 million dollars," he said proudly. "Seventy-five mil! Wow!" He laughed again, and it wasn't a black-humor laugh, but a genuine expression of the joy that comes from any great adventure—win or lose.

Needless to say, he had a dozen good ideas for rescuing the company, and each seemed to infuse him with energy. He ran through some of them with me, gleefully sorting out the best ideas like a kid picking through his Halloween candy.

His courage had once made him rich, and it still made him feel rich—or on the verge of it—even when he was busted down to nothing.

That's power over perception: choice in action.

The War for the Soul

My wife's father, Curtis Chapman, died while she was still young. In that era before camcorders, he'd recorded very little of his life that she could hold on to. With one notable exception. A diary.

It was the diary that he kept as a prisoner of war in a Nazi camp after his B-17 bomber was shot down.

My wife, Amy, and I have both read the diary many times. It is the story of his slow starvation at the hands of his captors. He was still alive at the end of the war, unlike some of his friends, but he was gaunt, emaciated, half-dead with hunger.

The diary was small, to make it easier to hide, and was pencil-written in compact, tight script. Its first pages talk about the terror of being shot down and captured, the harsh treatment during interrogation, and first impressions after arriving at a POW camp. After a number of weeks, though, as the hardships of cold, filth, and hunger mount, the subject matter changes. Abstract concepts fall away. Amy's father begins to write more about the ways that he and his friends—now made brothers by suffering—remake their world with the few possibilities that remain. They play cards, make their own games, learn new things from one another, share their lives. They give fancy names to their meager rations: "Spam à la King" and "Whipped Pommes de Terre." The world of their brotherhood becomes more real to them than their environment of privation.

Weeks become months, and hunger claws incessantly at their shrunken stomachs, and causes pain to shudder throughout their bodies, as they literally consume themselves. The diary changes again.

From this point until liberation, the diary is mostly about food. At first, it's just recollections about certain favorite foods and about pretending to eat them. Then it becomes heartbreakingly obsessive. Endless lists of foods. Menus. Dozens of recipes, some of which Amy's father remembers, and some of which came from his buddies. Meal plans. Alphabetical lists of foods. Foods organized by category. Favorite fruits. Favorites meats. Food, food, food, hunger. And finally, freedom.

When I first saw the diary, I was horrified by the fixation upon food, and incensed at the cruelty to these helpless men.

But finally I saw that they weren't helpless. In their vacuum of possibilities, they chose to *create* possibilities. They filled their horrible void with love of each other, hope for the future, and simple activities that were once too trivial to pursue. In their hunger, they ate mentally, creating fantasies of food that were so real that they were somehow fulfilling. These fantasies were all that was possible for them. But one possibility is all the heart needs.

These brave men: They were faced daily with the fear of death and were weakened beyond comprehension—but their spirits soared.

This year, Amy organized a reunion of these men. At first, some of them were scared to come. Too painful. It was that simple. They had memories burned into their brains that they were afraid to rekindle. The pain was too deep.

Sometimes, it feels as if all you'll ever do is weep, if just once you let yourself start. But these men had a love for one another even deeper in their hearts.

They were still at war, fighting the war between love and fear. This is the war that never ends. It is the war for the soul. It is the war we all fight, year after year.

In the end, they chose to come. They wanted to see each other, one last time, and talk about the war they'd won.

Choosing what's in your heart is hard. But it can happen at any age, after any hurt, to anyone.

I learned that the day I saw these men—these heroes of the soul—enter the room of the reunion, recognize each other, and embrace, as one.

A woman entered my office 3 days ago. She told me that she was at the end of her rope, and had lost all hope.

She was very successful, deeply involved in her career. But she'd been lonely all her life, and had never met a man she truly loved—until just a few months earlier.

And now her company wanted her to relocate. But the man she loved wouldn't leave, because of kids from a previous marriage.

Her life was hopeless, she said. Empty of options. Tragic.

For a moment, I flashed on images of other people who seemed to have no options. I saw Kate, walking up and down every corridor of the hospital, showing off her bicycle brake. I saw Vic, hugging his dad good-bye as he prepared to spend his first night alone, listening to the echoes of suffering. I saw Victor Frankl finding a flower in a death camp. And Amy's father, feasting on fantasies, when fantasy was all he had.

She seemed like a strong woman, and I knew she was intelligent.

We began to talk.

I don't have to tell you how the story ends. You already know.

You don't know whether she went for the job or the guy, of course—but that's not what the story is about, is it?

It's about choice, and knowing that it's always there. *Always.*

This woman found her choice. And so can you.

CHAPTER SIX

Power over Feelings, Power over Fate

T his guy had everything. I mean, *everything*. He was incredibly rich. Loved by millions. Talented beyond belief. Adored by a beautiful wife. In the prime of his life. And that was just the beginning.

He wasn't just another garden-variety billionaire. He had it better than that. No, he wasn't a movie star. Not a network anchorman, nor a presidential candidate. Not a world-famous novelist. He was the ultimate fantasy: a rock star.

Millions of people drove to work every day singing along with his songs. He was a fixture in the international culture. An idol. No dream was beyond his reach. And yet here he sat, crying his heart out about how bad he had it. My job was to sympathize.

Truth be told, it was easy for me to feel bad for him, because this man really was in pain. If you think his wealth and fame automatically protected him from suffering, you've missed the point of this book. The things in life that really hurt spare no one.

He was at war, fighting for his soul against fear, as are all of us who seek fulfillment and happiness. But he was losing—and his reptile was winning.

"I haven't had a creative thought in 2 damn years," he rasped, as slick tears slid down his cheeks. For him, that was worse than death. It was a walking death, devoid of the spark of inspiration that had fired the flame of his life. Since he'd been a child, he told me, he'd been able to slip the bonds of time and space and travel to the formless landscape of creativity, where there is no fear or regret, no past or future, but just the magical feeling of making something out of nothing, in a moment that somehow stands still. That was his happiness.

Some psychologists call this feeling "the zone of altered consciousness." Prominent happiness researcher Mihaly Csikzentmihalyi simply calls it "flow," and considers it vital to happiness. Virtually everyone who has studied it agrees that it is a state of heightened consciousness, joyous and productive, that is akin to a deeply spiritual experience. This state is commonly achieved not only by artists, but by anyone who's able to become totally absorbed in what they're doing. This often includes inventors, mathematicians, meditators, and even athletes. Most ordinary people, in fact, pay occasional visits to this zone, but only those who lead from their spirit can reach it at will.

Even so, this blessing, like all others, carries a curse. The zone of creativity can be isolating and exhausting. Even more dangerous, it can create rewards of money and status that ultimately destroy the state itself. Success is just too seductive. It tempts almost everyone who achieves it to abandon the qualities that first created it. This is the failure of success.

Oftentimes, creative people who achieve success rebel against its seduction by cloistering themselves in humble surroundings. But can a rock star? How do you stay humble with 20,000 people chanting your name? How do you cloister yourself in a spotlight?

"I've got to get out of this tour," the rock star said, quietly but passionately. "It's killing me."

He wasn't exaggerating. Ever since he'd embarked on a 10-country tour, 3 months earlier, his appetite for escape had taken over his life. He was trying to flee by drinking more than a fifth of Scotch whiskey every day and using cocaine and heroin. He'd abstained from using crack cocaine, he informed me with some pride, and had thus far just snorted heroin, instead of injecting it, but the drugs and booze were taking a cumulative toll. He was jaundiced from an encroaching liver disease and had lost so much weight that his skin hung in drips and drops off his face, as if he were melting from the inside out. He was suffering from heart arrythmia, clinical depression, and recurrent infections of his sinuses and lungs that overpowered his debilitated immune system and spiraled into raging fevers. Even so, he was captive to the notion that the show must go on.

Originally, he'd lurched into his indulgence as a rebellion against the rigid schedule and the pretentiousness of the tour, but the vices had gained a life of their own, as all vices do.

"I think you should take a medical leave of absence," I told him— and he looked at me as if I were insane.

"Do you know what that would *cost* me?" he wailed.

"Less than dying. If you count lost earnings."

"It would *cost* me about $15 million in concert fees, and another $10 million in record sales. Add on another two or three million in legal fees, after the concert promoters sue me. It might cost me my recording con- tract, and my fans would kill me. Plus—*plus*—my manager, my agent, my lawyer, and my label president would go nuts. They're the ones run- ning the show," he said bitterly. "I'm just the poster boy."

"Lot of people depend on you?"

"You have no idea."

"Feel powerless?"

He just looked at me with his big, famous eyes, searching my face for pity.

So there we sat. What could I do? He had abdicated his personal power, and that is a sin against the soul. It's poison for proactivity, a sense of freedom, and courage, and without these qualities, there can be no happiness.

Like the rock star and everyone else, you were born with personal power. It is the almost indefinable vital force that enables you to be happy with your life, even when it's hard. It comes from the combined power of your intellect and spirit, working in perfect harmony, and it gives you your ultimate strength in life—the strength to manage your own emotions and not let them be dictated by outside forces.

When your personal power is at its peak, it not only enables you to accept your fate—whatever that fate may be—but also helps you *create* that fate.

Thus, personal power is your power over feelings, and your power over fate.

When your sense of personal power is strong, you're not afraid. You know that you can take whatever life can dish out. You know that other people can affect you but that no one can control you.

Your personal power is the root, psychological source of your physical and emotional energies. It lies at the core of your being, and it makes you want to get up every morning and tackle the day. It's personal power that enables you to make choices, and it's personal power that gives you the courage to feel the love that drives fear away.

There are other words for personal power. Probably the best is "character." You could also call it strength, individuality, heart, will, or even charisma. All of these elements are part of personal power, but the whole of it is greater than the sum of its parts.

Ultimately, personal power is about doing. It's a moving, changing entity, like wind.

Because it's about doing, it consists of two active forces: taking responsibility and taking action.

It consists, quite simply, of realizing that your life belongs to you and you alone, and then doing something about it.

Sound easy?

It was just about impossible for the rock star. He was convinced that other people had taken control of his life, and that he was helpless, frozen in place.

This passive attitude had mired him deeply into the fear-driven happiness traps. As his personal power had begun to evaporate, he had traded his values of creativity and freedom for money. When that had made him miserable, he'd tried to force himself to be happy through the dubious pleasures of drugs and alcohol. He kept telling himself that he could overcome his weakness for substances—quit cold-turkey—but that was just his vanity talking. He was stuck.

Now he was a pawn, driven by addictions and controlled by the whims of greedy men.

"You've gotta help me," he said. But it wasn't a plea; it was a demand.

He saw himself as a victim and blamed the corporate managers who controlled him. But he still saw himself as a star, and therefore felt entitled to be rescued—by The Great Doctor Me.

"We need to do a lot of work," I told him.

He nodded.

We got busy. We made some progress that day.

But not enough. That night, he went home and put a gun in his mouth.

Not Everyone Gets It

I'll repeat that, for emphasis: *Not everyone gets it.*

I sincerely hope that you are trying to get the points that I'm making in this book—trying to really feel them and use them. It's so easy to read a book like this and just be entertained by the stories, remember some of the aphorisms, and then let it all slide into oblivion.

It's especially easy to not get the hard stuff—the painful material that challenges your beliefs. For a lot of people, this chapter will be nothing but hard stuff. Nothing is harder than dumping the false beliefs that destroy personal power.

To do this, you'll probably have to let go of beliefs that have long brought you comfort. You've likely learned to think of them as allies in your struggle to survive, but they're your enemies.

In the quest to build personal power, there are four extremely common beliefs that seem comforting, but are deadly foes. They are:

1. I've been victimized.
2. I'm entitled to more.
3. I'll be rescued.
4. Someone else is to blame.

Those are the beliefs that had destroyed the rock star's personal power, and—if you'll be honest and really try to get it—you'll see that they're probably also beliefs that are holding down your personal power.

Maybe you're thinking, "Whoa! Hold on! I'm not a drunk and a druggie. (And I *have* been victimized, and I know exactly who's to blame.)"

If so, maybe you'll be able to relate to a more prosaic illustration, one I've encountered about 200 times. Here it is: A husband walks into my office—or it could just as easily be a wife—and says, in so many words, "My wife is driving me crazy! She does nothing but nag, nag, nag. I love her, and I want to try to stay together, but I swear to God I can't take much more. She knows it pushes my buttons—I've asked her to lay off a million times—but she does it anyway."

My first question to him is, "Does she have a point?"

He probably replies with something like, "Sometimes she has a point—but it's the way she makes it that's driving me crazy."

I'll ask, "She has a lot of power over you?"

"Oh, yeah," he'll say, "way too much. Everybody wonders how I put up with it."

At this point, he'll expect me to jump on his bandwagon, validate his feelings, and give him some good antiwife ammunition to take home. He'll want me to say, "Sounds like your wife has a problem."

But I say, "It sounds like you've got a problem."

At that point, often as not, I'll lose him. Then I'll have to try to reel him back in.

He'll be livid: "*I've* got a problem? She's the one that nags!"

"But you're the one who has a problem with it."

"Who wouldn't?"

"Millions of guys have wives who nag, but it's not a big issue for them."

"I'm not one of those millions of guys."

"You could be. You could rise above it, to a level you don't even know exists."

He'll look distrustful. I've seen the look 200 times. But he'll be curious.

"How?"

Then I'll tell him about the life-changing quarter-second, when he has the choice of changing his perception. I'll tell him about appreciation, and how it can literally reprogram his brain and stop the automatic reactivity of the fear-and-anger response. I'll tell him about the immense strength of his personal power, and how it can help him rise above anger, even when his wife is nagging. And I'll tell him about the four primary beliefs that kill personal power.

By this time, if he's not starting to get it, he'll just tune me out. To him, I'll just be one more person who doesn't understand him (a touchy-feely psychobabbler who's probably afraid to stand up to his own wife!). If that's the case, there's not much I can do. Not everyone gets it.

If he is starting to get it, though, he'll probably ask a good question, such as, "You mean I should accept it?"

"No. You don't have to accept it. Nagging is not good. It's not polite. It's not constructive. You just have to find a way to keep it from pushing your buttons."

He'll tell me how long he's had his buttons, probably connecting them with something in his past, most likely a nagging mother.

I'll remind him that he's here to change his life, not relive it.

He might take a last stab at convincing me that it's his wife who needs to change, not him.

But I'll tell him that it's him I'm trying to help, and that he can change his life without changing his wife. And even if she does change, there will always be somebody else pushing his nag button.

What he needs to quit doing, I'll say, is giving away his power. I'll tell him that every time his wife nags now, he willingly bequeaths all his personal power to her—hands it over on a silver platter. When he reacts automatically, without bringing his spirit and intellect to the situation, she becomes the one who's in charge of how he feels, not him.

"Who do you want running your emotions," I'll ask, "her or you?" There was probably a time in grade school, I might say, when somebody could get under his skin by saying something as absurd as "My dad can beat up your dad." But as he matured, he learned to let that kind of nonsense slide. He took power then, and he can do it again.

It's amazing, I'll mention, how many people take full responsibility for their own behavior, but refuse to take responsibility for their feelings. They think their feelings are a force of nature, wild and uncontrollable. Not so.

Here's a fact of life, a good one: Just as you can change your behavior, you can also change your feelings. The same forces of personal power influence both.

"But shouldn't I stand up for myself?" he might ask.

"Refusing to engage in the same old craziness is the ultimate form of standing up for yourself."

"What will happen if I *don't* let my wife push my buttons?"

"Something different." That's all I can ever promise.

But I'll tell you what usually happens. More often than not, if you do a button-ectomy on yourself—and no longer react automatically—people will stop pushing that button. They will change.

Part of the reason they will change is that they won't have to push your buttons anymore to try to get through to you. When you stop responding with your usual autopilot, fight-flee-freeze reaction, you're far more likely to give them the kind of feedback they need. The escalation of aggression ends. Old patterns change.

Another reason people will change is that they'll simply respect you more. When you make the first move and overcome your pride and anger, you stand taller in the estimation of others. You seem wiser and kinder. And when people who are wise and kind speak, everybody listens.

But having someone else change is not the real prize. The real prize is the feeling you get inside when you learn to take responsibility for your own feelings. That feeling of personal power is yours, and no one can destroy it but you. If you nurture it, it's untouchable, unshakable, eternal.

The more you exercise this power, the stronger it becomes. At its zenith, it is so potent a force that it's capable of protecting you not only from the emotional assaults of others, but from the tragedies of life itself.

Even with this protection, of course, much of the pain of life will remain, because life without pain is just a dream, unreal, and ultimately empty. But this remaining pain will never be all that's left of life, as it so often is for the defenseless people who abdicate their personal power and let others dictate the terms of their existence.

If this abdication occurs, pain will swallow you whole. You will cease to be yourself.

If you allow this to happen, you will, in a real way, have killed yourself.

The Rock Star

"My husband was born to play in sleazy little bars," the rock star's wife told me the morning after his suicide attempt. "You hear a lot of these rockers," she said, "and they're trying to sound all badass, but they're nothing but rich kids in dirty clothes." Her husband, she said, was "the real deal." Born in poverty, raised by a neglectful single mother, he'd been a genuine rebel, preaching the gospel of individualism and antimaterialism. But he'd preached it so well that he'd gotten rich from it, and that had been his undoing.

He'd found himself living a life that contradicted his values, and that murders personal power. If you don't believe in what you're doing but still devote all your life's energies to it, your personal power disappears. It's not just other people and the cruelty of life that beat down the internal vital force of personal power. Often as not, we do it to ourselves—willingly, consciously, and gleefully. We just don't have the courage to live up to our values. We give in a little here, a little there, cut some corners, sell ourselves short—and gradually our internal balance of power shifts from strength to weakness. We stop making our own rules and owning our own days. We begin to hide behind victimization, entitlement, rescue, and blame. We say, "Oh, that's life—you do what you have to."

But that's not life. It's death. The death of the soul.

"Where's your husband now?" I asked the rock star's beautiful wife, as she stared glumly out my window.

"Still in the hospital, under suicide watch."

"How did you keep him from pulling the trigger?"

"I . . ." her voice caught, "begged."

"Have they got him on antidepressants?"

"By the truckload."

"Good." He needed a full-spectrum approach, including appropriate medication. His body, sick with addiction and neurochemical imbalance, had taken over his mind. Until he reclaimed his health, he'd never have a chance to feel like his old self, and would probably try once again to kill the empty new self he'd created. Repairing his biochemistry, however, would only take a few weeks. Then the real work would start.

His real work would be to again become the self he'd left behind. That self was the source of his personal power.

I know that many psychology books talk about finding yourself, as if that's the Holy Grail. But I've met many people who have found themselves, gained a great deal of personal insight—and were still absolutely miserable. Finding yourself is just the beginning. The important thing is *being* yourself. Acting like yourself. That's harder. But it's that path that leads to personal power.

Being yourself requires courage. Sweat. Sacrifice. It means forgetting about what others want you to be and being who you are. It means living up to your values.

Your values are the individualized beliefs that make you *you*. Without them, you—as an individual—cease to exist.

I told the rock star's wife that I didn't think her husband could ever crawl out of the hole he'd dug for himself until he started living up to his own personal values—the spiritual and moral qualities he had that commanded esteem. At first, she wasn't even sure what I was talking about. People don't often discuss values these days. In our homogeneous, media-dominated culture, there's a blithe general assumption that almost all of us share the same basic values—or should. But that's absurd. We're vastly different from each other, and when we fail to act on these differences in our own lives, or fail to honor them in the lives of others, we assault the source of all personal power.

Personal power is *personal*; yours comes from you alone, and anybody who encroaches on your individuality diminishes your power. For example, I love to be adventurous, but there are a lot of people who might consider some of the things I do to be just frivolous thrill seeking. Good for them! I'd never dream of trying to wrest that value away from them. It's a perfectly reasonable value. And so is mine.

Have you given much thought lately to what your values are? You should, because if you don't know your values, you won't be able to take responsibility for what you do, and build your personal power.

If you don't know what you stand for, desire, and admire, your personal power will eventually degenerate into a chaotic, undirected, entropic force, which will scatter to the four winds.

The table on the opposite page will help you think about your values.

If you're thinking right now that they all sound so good that they must be part of your fundamental personality, you're kidding yourself. Nobody embodies all of these values—and nobody should. If they did, they'd just be a cardboard cutout, or a character in a cheap romance novel. Look at the list again, and pick out the top five or six that are most

WHAT DO YOU VALUE MOST?

Adventurousness	Dependability	Kindness
Aggressiveness	Empathy	Logic
Artistry	Extroversion	Love
Attractiveness	Faithfulness	Loyalty
Boldness	Fitness	Perceptiveness
Charity	Flexibility	Pleasure
Charm	Health	Reverence
Cheerfulness	Helpfulness	Security
Civility	Honesty	Simplicity
Cleanliness	Humility	Thrift
Compassion	Humor	Trustworthiness
Courage	Intelligence	Wealth
Creativity	Inventiveness	Wisdom

applicable. *That's* you. At the very least, it's a vision of what you could be.

Be honest, and try hard to decide exactly what your core values are, because when people identify their values, it gives their lives focus, and gives them a sense of security during times of chaos and confusion.

When people live up to their values, it gives them a sense of purpose, peace of mind, and fulfillment—all necessary ingredients for happiness. It allows their spirit to lead in the dance of the spirit and the reptile.

A rabbi once told me that he hoped his enemies would come to his funeral, just to celebrate. It would mean that his life had stood for something.

However, when people fail to live up to their values, the first thing they feel is disappointment in themselves, which creates a lot of stress. But that's not the end of it. Often as not, to try to fill in the holes that this disappointment creates, they fall into the happiness traps. They try to find happiness through money, pleasure, worldly power, or some other fruitless source. When these attempts fail, they generally begin to feel like victims: "I've tried so hard! But the deck was stacked against me!" They feel entitled to more, and look for someone to rescue them. When their rescuers fail, they blame them—or blame the whole world, or even God.

As their energy fades, they again try to draw upon their well of personal power, the power that once made them feel whole and happy. But now this power is diluted! It's been weakened by victimization, entitlement, rescue, and blame. These disempowering qualities are the absolute antithesis of personal power, which consists of taking responsibility and taking action.

Victimization, Entitlement, Rescue, and *Blame* are so common, and so often tied together, that I've begun to describe them with an acronym. I call them the VERBs.

I told the rock star's wife that her husband was dying from a bad case of the VERBs. He'd traded his values for the VERBs, I said, and it had been a deadly exchange.

She got it. Right away.

But the rock star didn't get it, at least not at first, when I visited him in the hospital. He fought with the fury of a drowning man to hang on to his VERBs, because he saw them as his last hope for making sense of his life.

He was too smart and too tough, however, to hang on to them forever.

Do you remember the learned helplessness experiments, in which most of the dogs learned to sit helplessly in their cages despite electric shocks? Some of these dogs—about one-third—*refused* to be passive, and found the escape route. Interestingly, among the group of dogs who refused to be victimized, a great many had come from the dog pound.

They were tougher and more resilient than the lab-raised dogs. The rock star—a product of neglect and poverty—was a classic "pound dog." He was a survivor.

That might sound like a strange thing to call a man who had tried to kill himself. But it wasn't his true self he'd wanted dead. It was the self that had betrayed his values and made his life miserable.

He went to war against this false self. He was an extremist by nature, so this war was often bitter and bloody. As he'd expected, the men who were making money off him—some of them extremely powerful—fought him every step of the way.

But after a while, he no longer had to fight against his false self. He just . . . let it go. He knew it wasn't him, and he simply lost interest in it.

As his personal power returned, he cut loose the people who were hanging on him, and simplified his career. No more stadiums. No more high-pressure recording contracts. He went back to the small clubs he loved, and wrote the songs—not often popular—that were close to his heart.

Of course, he took a tremendous financial hit. You wouldn't even want to know how much money he sacrificed.

These days, years later, he's more or less in the "What ever happened to . . . ?" category. He plays little dives and seedy, retro nightclubs, and every once in awhile he releases a CD on a minor label, run by executives who don't make him tour.

Occasionally, his name will come up, and people will tend to say things along the lines of, "Poor guy. He had it all—and lost it."

He had *nothing*. He *lost* nothing.

He beat back the VERBs, lived up to his own lofty values, and won back his life. If you saw him today, you'd see a man who's happy and creative, wise and kind, in love with his wife and in love with life. If ever I've known a winner, it's him.

The VERBs

Victimization

Early in my career, a brave woman changed my view of victimization forever. She was a former prisoner of the Soviet gulag who had spent 12 years in the 1950s and 1960s in concentration camps. She'd been starved, beaten, and humiliated, and had lost two fingers to frostbite.

At one point during a counseling session, I made a reference to her as a concentration camp victim. Big mistake!

"Victim!" she cried. "I am not a victim. I survived!"

Good point. Surviving that ordeal was the pride of her life—an epic victory of her spirit—and she wasn't about to let anybody look at her as a "poor old thing."

Of course, she was, by the usual definition of the word, a victim. But she didn't let it define her. She had been hurt, but that hurt wasn't *her*. It was over—and she was still here, proud, defiant, and full of heart. She had been a victim without giving in to victimization, and that had put her hurt in the past.

Many people just can't do this. They carry their hurt forever. They begin to define themselves as their pain, and lose touch with their true selves. This rots the foundation of their personal power and warps their view of reality.

The ugly transition from victim to victimization starts with fear. It begins when people give in to the lightning-fast fear response, and freeze. They often stay frozen in this fear forever, constantly reliving their torment.

The most common instance of this plight is feeling victimized by one's childhood. This condition is pandemic.

It is not unusual to have a hard childhood. By its very nature, childhood is our most vulnerable time, and often this vulnerability is exploited and abused.

But childhood ends.

The memories don't, though. Old pain is still pain, and the recollections of it will always hurt. These days, however, it's widely considered a psychological pathology to still have painful childhood memories. Painful memories are supposed to be validated, explored, processed, and resolved—thus alchemizing them into happy memories.

Now, *that's* crazy. There's no pathology in being troubled by a troublesome past. It's normal, a sign of health. It makes you human. As Dr. Martin Seligman has said, "It's as if some idiot raised the ante on what it takes to be a normal human being."

Life hurts. If it doesn't hurt some of the time, it's not life.

But you can't allow yourself to get wrapped up in this hurt, constantly reliving it, fearing the future and grieving the past. That's victimization.

Other people can hurt you, but only you can victimize yourself.

Feeling victimized usually feels comforting at first. It's a sanctuary of self-involvement. It paves the path to indulgence and creates community with other victims. But it kills you with kindness. You get trapped by its secondary benefits and begin to enjoy it. Researcher Charles Sykes calls this "wearing the velvet manacles."

When people begin to enjoy their victimization, they often base their lives on it. They go straight from their Victims of Anonymity Anonymous meeting to a support group for Parents of Kids Who Are Hooked on Phonics. Then they visit their lawyer to check on their suit against McDonald's (for making them fat) and end the day by calling mom to complain—collect, of course.

As victimization becomes a way of life, injuries begin to appear everywhere. I've worked with victims of unattractiveness (or "pretty oppression," as it was explained to me), and I've worked with people who are victims of being "just another pretty face." I've worked with victims of being the middle child, and the oldest child, and the baby of the family. I've even worked with a woman who was emotionally crushed when her husband quit drinking, because she was no longer welcome at her codependency group. She "found healing," however, by starting her own group—of recovering codependents.

Victimization is more common than ever before, partly because of two multibillion-dollar professions: the psychology profession and the legal profession. Every day, lawyers and psychologists convince thousands of people that they have been victimized.

Psychologists see their clients as victims because psychology is based on the traditional medical model, which assumes that people are healthy until some outside pathogen (such as a germ) subverts them. In psychology, the most common "pathogen" is presumed to be the dysfunctional parent—followed by the unsympathetic spouse, the demanding boss, the ungrateful child, and fate itself.

Another reason psychologists see patients as victims is because it's the patient who pays the bill. The customer is always right. Plus, if the patient is the victim, guess who gets to ride in on the big white horse?

Victimization got a big boost during the narcissistic, 1970s Me Decade, with the widespread acceptance of the theory that drinking too much alcohol is a physical disease. There's truth to this, but what a Pandora's box! It helped create recognized and reimbursable diseases such as Internet addiction, love addiction, UFO abduction post-traumatic stress disorder, debtor addiction (overuse of credit cards), and telephone scatalogia (I'll let you figure that one out).

Often, diseases of this nature are invoked as legal defenses by psychology's primary codependent in the victimization industry: the members of the American Bar Association.

It's not your imagination: There are far more lawyers in the world than there once were, and there are far more in America than anywhere else—many of them looking for victims to represent. In 1950, there were 200,000 lawyers in America, but now 200,000 new lawyers graduate in every 5-year period. America has 281 lawyers for every 100,000 people—compared to 82 in England and 11 in Japan—which results in America having 70 percent of all the lawyers in the world.

This has resulted in an explosion of lawsuits and created whole new groups of victims. For example, the San Francisco Giants were sued for passing out Father's Day gifts to men only. A psychology professor sued for sexual harassment because of the presence of mistletoe at a Christmas party. A psychic was awarded $986,000 when a doctor's CT scan impaired her psychic ability. (And you thought *you* had problems!)

Thousands of criminal cases have also metastasized the definition of victimization. One man who murdered two people was found not responsible for the crime due to his sleepwalking disorder (even though he had to drive 15 miles to do the killing). In a rather famous case, a judge argued that he had committed extortion and had threatened to kidnap his girlfriend due to his Clerambault-Kandinsky syndrome (or irresistible lovesickness). In Milwaukee, a teenage girl pled not guilty to shooting another girl in an argument over a leather coat, on the grounds that she suffered from "cultural psychosis," which made her believe that problems can be solved with violence. My favorite legal argument came from a very prominent psychology professor, who said that a mass murderer was not guilty because it is impossible, in this beautiful world, for any *sane* person to choose to do wrong.

Well, my God! That lets a few of us off the hook, doesn't it?

The psychology professor contended that in this particular case, "postmodern justice" should be applied. Excuse my language, but what in hell is postmodern justice? On second thought, don't bother to excuse my language; I suffer from chronic profanitosis, and I have the right to swear.

A third major culprit in the modern cult of victimization is the government. When bloated bureaucracies can't find victims that need help, they often create them. One of the best examples is the exaggeration of the victimization of Vietnam War veterans. If you're like me, when you first heard the exaggerations about Vietnam vet dysfunction, you swallowed them hook, line, and sinker.

Shortly after the war ended, the government propagated the notion, using their own studies, that one out of three Vietnam vets was homeless, that more had died from suicide than had died in the war, that 26 percent suffered from post-traumatic stress disorder, that many were violent, and that an inordinate number of them had become addicted to drugs and alcohol. This prompted enormous increases in funding to the Veterans Administration (VA), the Department of Housing and Urban Development, the Drug Enforcement Agency, and innumerable smaller bureaucracies, such as the Homeless Chronically Mentally Ill Program.

After all, these poor, screwed-up vets needed help! They were chronically mentally ill! Homeless! Addicted! Dangerous!

But subsequent, larger studies showed that this supposedly well-meant characterization of the vets was hogwash. The vets weren't much different from their peers. A large study by the Centers for Disease Control (which had no financial stake in the outcome) showed that the percentage of vets with post-traumatic stress disorder really wasn't 26 percent, but was about 2 percent. Despite this, the VA still embraced the study showing 26 percent, even though this study was only one-tenth as large as the other. They said that the very small study "proved the need" for construction of more vet centers, more funding, and more jobs.

Many other large, follow-up studies also showed that the vets had no significant excess of homelessness, substance abuse, violent behavior, mental illness, or suicide.

Nonetheless, the public stigma of victimization had been attached: The vets were sick, ticking time bombs. This ruined many lives.

But the funding lives on!

Of course, there was never any funding to study the vets who had suffered trauma but still thrived. What would be the value of that?

It's easy to blame the government, the legal profession, and the psychology profession for expanding victimization. They are guilty.

But only one person has the final say in making you feel like a victim. It's you, of course.

There is an antidote to feeling victimized. Because victimization is rooted in fear, the antidote to victimization is the same as the antidote to fear: appreciation.

The best way to get over feeling sorry for yourself is to appreciate yourself. If you sincerely love yourself and are truly proud of what you are, it becomes very difficult to feel like a victim. Sure, you have challenges. People have hurt you. But look at the goodness that's still in your heart! Look at the strength of your spirit! The intelligence of your mind! You are a victim of no one.

The ultimate blessing of human existence lies right at your feet: love of your true self.

Accept this blessing. Do this one thing, and happiness—even with pain still a part of it—can be yours.

Entitlement

Entitlement is victimization waiting to happen.

Even so, feeling entitled is extremely common. Most of our current government spending is on "the entitlements." Consumerism—two-thirds of our economy—is founded on making people feel entitled to have things they don't already have. The rich feel entitled to keep what they have, and the poor feel entitled to try to take it.

But despite its entrenchment in our society, entitlement is contrary to human nature. The human mind, body, and spirit thrive on struggle and challenge, just as a muscle thrives on exercise. Satisfaction without effort doesn't create happiness. It creates only dissipation, alienation, boredom, weakness, and a sense of worthlessness.

Even infants, weeks old, prefer to hold their own bottles, apparently to satisfy the instinct to grasp. Infants have many other instincts that also propel them to reach out, explore, and take power over their own lives. People are not born passive.

However, as we grow older, we become accustomed to the care of others, and our natural instinct to do things for ourselves can begin to wither. Our human weakness tells us: Sit back, relax, and let Mom take care of the problems.

Then one of two things happens. Either somebody else does take care of things—or they don't. If they do, we're tempted to let them keep it up. If they don't, we're tempted to think we've been short-changed and are entitled to more. Both these temptations are insidious. They undermine responsibility and subvert personal power.

Unfortunately, as personal power shrinks, the VERBs expand. Eventually, the trap springs shut. We become too weak to get what we think we deserve (and that just makes us want it all the more).

I often see this happen to rich kids. They grow up in the condition that I call "enriched deprivation." They have so much that everything becomes meaningless. There's nothing left to yearn for, so they lose their power to grow and grasp. They feel entitled to luxury and come to expect it—but expectations, as you may recall, are one of the worst enemies of happiness. These kids become weak, jaded, and ungrateful. Even as adults, they're often nothing but trust fund babies. They not only lack a sense of self-esteem, they lack a sense of self. They often become vulnerable to the happiness traps, particularly unbridled pleasure, since they have the time and money to pursue it.

I once knew a young man who was so frightened by the emptiness of his pampered life, and so full of self-contempt for his own profligacy—fueled by a $10,000-a-month allowance—that he fled into heavy drug use. When he piled up his Aston Martin, his dad wanted to buy him a bus pass, but mom gave him a Porsche and said, "If he dies, I want him to go out in style." Sadly, that's exactly what happened. Her words, painfully prophetic, haunt her still.

It doesn't have to be like this. I remember another rich teenage kid who was taking every drug he could get his hands on and was driving his dad crazy. His sisters were in trouble, too; one had a serious eating disorder and the other was a compulsive shoplifter. They were all miserable, and mom wasn't much better off—she drank all afternoon at the country club just to feel good enough to get drunk at night.

Dad was the one who came to see me. He looked harried, as if two people were calling out to him from different directions. He'd sweated his life away, he said, to keep his family happy, but they were always whining for more. He'd begun to spend even more time at work, just to stay away from them.

"I'm doing my part as the provider," he said, "and look where it's gotten me."

"Sounds like you've got a problem."

"No kidding. They're just impossible."

"I mean, it sounds like *you've* got a problem."

He threw an exasperated look at me. "You don't think *they've* got the problem?"

"Sure, they have problems—but so do you. You've got the most common dad problem in the world: You think that if you cover all the bills, it's okay to ignore your family."

"I ignore them because they're a mess."

"And part of the reason they're a mess is because you ignore them."

"That's their problem."

"It's your problem, too."

"How so?"

"Because you're suffering from it."

He must have sat there thinking about it for 5 minutes. I stayed quiet. It takes time to let go of the VERBs, because they're so comforting—even as they destroy you.

After a while, I said, "Family problems can often be solved when any one member steps up and takes responsibility. Do you want to be the one?"

"Why me?"

"Because you can't make them change. You can only make yourself change, and I think you've got a problem. All you give is money, because you're afraid to give love."

"I wouldn't know . . ." he sighed, and I could hear years of loneliness in the whisper of his breath, ". . . where to start."

"Write your wife a memo."

I wasn't kidding. This guy was famous for his memos. He ran his company with long memos, and he had them down to an art. It was one of his strengths.

He did it. Six drafts. With each draft, he learned a little more about himself. He told his wife that he'd been afraid of intimacy and had tried to show his love with his money. He told her that he needed her to help him fight his fear of closeness, and asked if she would go to couples counseling with him.

He said he loved her and the kids more than his career, and promised to start acting like it—no matter what anyone else in the family did.

It was an honest and beautiful letter, straight from his heart, and his wife was moved by his courage.

They both worked hard. They did all the scary things they thought they'd lost the strength to do. And they changed. He stopped hiding behind his work and she stopped hiding behind the bottle.

The kids were shocked. Frightened by it. Challenged. And blasted out of their own hiding places forever. The daughter with the eating disorder needed counseling and medication (a serotonin enhancer) to get better, but the other two kids just needed their mom and dad. When they had that, their psychological "diseases" vanished.

A family changed.

But more important than that, a man changed. A woman changed. Three children changed.

Even in a family, when you find your personal power, you find it alone.

This is not tragic. It's beautiful. But it's a kind of beauty you'll never understand until the day you finally feel it.

Rescue

When trouble strikes and people take the fork in the road that leads to fear, they often cry out for help.

In our current institution-dominated, touchy-feely society, in which self-reliance is on the decline, this cry for help has been glorified. It's considered by many psychologists to be the first step toward healing—a sign of openness and of being in touch with one's inner child.

But in real life, it's disastrous.

When you don't take the fork that leads to fear, but instead count on your own spirit and intellect to pull you through, *that's* when it's smart to look for help. With a clear head and strong heart, you can get the kind of assistance you need without giving up your own personal power. But when you're frozen in fear, your cry for help is really a cry for rescue— and rescue is insidious.

Even if you get rescued (which is not a sure thing), you're still left with a nagging reminder that you're not enough—and that when your next problem hits, you're going to have to flee from it until another rescuer arrives.

The desire for rescue is one of the most well-established phenomena in history. From the days of Sir Lancelot, to Robin Hood, to the Lone

Ranger, to Superman, to Robocop, it's a concept that just won't die. Most of the melodramas ever made have been about a damsel in distress, rescued by a knight in shining armor (or a Kevlar vest). Everybody's always wanted salvation without sweat.

Many of us are looking for rescue without even knowing it. All we know is that something is missing from our lives and that we can't possibly be happy until we have it. As a general rule, men look more to money for rescue, and women look more to relationships. I've met thousands of men who are certain they will be happy just as soon as they get that next promotion, make their first million, or buy that boat. And I've met thousands of women who are convinced that they can never be truly happy until they have a husband, or work out their relationship with their mother, their sister, or someone else.

Of course, this rarely works. The new promotion is never enough ("It's just a stepping-stone!"). And the new husband always falls short ("If only he were as romantic as before!").

One of the terrible problems with rescue is that the rescuer is almost always idealized, since the rescuer started out as a product of the victim's imagination in the first place. The rescuing husband-to-be isn't just a man, he's Mr. Perfect. The rescuing promotion isn't just a job, it's the opportunity of a lifetime. Rescuers ride in on big white horses, not donkeys.

There's nothing wrong with rescue when you're genuinely helpless: If you're drowning, yell for the lifeguard. But for day-to-day emotional problems, rescue isn't the answer.

If it were, the members of the psychology profession would be able to work wonders. After all, psychologists and psychiatrists are the most highly trained people in the world at emotional rescue. But even psychologists can't achieve very much when they use only their own powers. They mostly rely upon *your* powers.

This was proven all the way back in 1975, when three cutting-edge psychologists (Luborsky, Singer, and Luborsky) shocked the world of psychology by announcing the momentous "dodo bird verdict." These psychologists were trying to figure out which brand of psychotherapy was really the best when they discovered, to their astonishment, that there *was* no best approach. Thus, they borrowed a phrase from *Alice in Wonderland*, in which a contest for supremacy ended in a dodo bird's verdict: "Everyone has won—so all must have prizes!"

When they released their findings, the psychology community was scandalized. The dodo bird verdict! Applied to the exact science of psychology?

It was bad enough that the dodo bird verdict devalued the private predilections of each individual school of psychology, but the real damage came from the study's subtext: If no single therapy is superior, then some other healing factor is at work, elevating the effectiveness of the poor approaches to that of the good ones.

That factor was proven to be—of all things!—the patients themselves. *They* were the primary healing force—and if some of them used Jungian analysis while others engaged in primal therapy, it really didn't matter.

This led to the concept called patient as change agent, which means, translated from psycho-jargon, that patients usually heal themselves, with only ancillary help from therapists. How many therapists does it take to change a lightbulb? Only one, if the lightbulb really wants to change.

It was even demonstrated, in two different studies in the 1990s, that psychology self-help books were just as effective as psychological counseling. Furthermore, it didn't appear to make much difference which self-help book was used—one was about as effective as the next (until the publication of this book, of course).

Not only that, a study in 1990 showed that computer-provided therapy was just as effective in the treatment of depression as professional counseling. The horror! Replaced by a machine! That was for factory workers!

Of course, you don't hear much from the psychology profession about the patient as the primary healing force. In most psychology books, the therapist is the hero. As an African proverb says, "Until lions have their historians, all tales of hunting will glorify the hunter."

In fact, a dirty little secret of psychology is that many psychologists tend to not only see themselves as heroes and their patients as helpless, but also see their patients as more troubled than they really are. They often even see pathology where none exists. This was demonstrated by two fascinating recent experiments. In one, eight "eminently normal" people were placed in a psychiatric hospital and asked to behave in their usual, healthy manner. None were discovered by any of the doctors to be a fake. Instead, doctors labeled their normal behavior as sick. For example, one "patient" who took notes during the experiment was categorized as engaging in pathological "writing behavior," though no one ever looked at his notes.

In another experiment, a group of therapists listened to a tape recording of what they were told was a counseling session. In actuality, the tape featured an actor who was told to play the role of a relaxed, confident man who was free of any psychological problems. However, 43 percent of the therapists labeled him as psychotic or neurotic, and another 19 percent said that he had adjustment problems.

There's nothing new about psychologists seeing normal behavior as deviant. Sigmund Freud claimed that every person alive was "psychotic at one point or another, in a greater or lesser degree," and that everyone was "only approximately normal." During the height of Freudianism, in the 1950s, doctors conducting a psychological survey of 1,500 people declared that only one in five was mentally healthy. In the 1970s, a prominent figure at the National Institute of Mental Health (NIMH) proclaimed that "almost no family in the nation is entirely free of mental disorders" and estimated that approximately 25 percent of all Americans "exhibit deviant mental behavior related to schizophrenia." As late as 2001, the NIMH claimed that 30 percent of all Americans needed mental

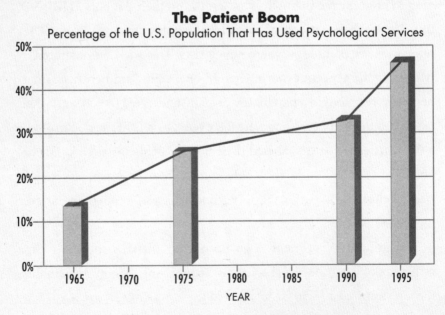

The Patient Boom
Percentage of the U.S. Population That Has Used Psychological Services

From *Manufacturing Victims*, by Dr. Tana Dineen, Robert Davies Multimedia Publishing, 1996.

What Happy People Know

health care every year. But in 2002, a new survey showed the real number was about half that—thus "curing" about 19 million people each year.

This presumed epidemic of mental illness has triggered an explosion in the number of therapists in America. The country now has more therapists than firefighters or mail carriers, and has twice as many therapists as dentists or pharmacists.

The charts on the opposite page and below, "The Patient Boom" and "The Doctor Boom," document the recent bloating of the psychology industry to its current $5-billion-per-year status.

Many of these psychologists make their living by riding to the rescue of the same patient again and again, billing cycle after billing cycle. A recent study showed that about 16 percent of American psychology patients account for almost two-thirds of all psychology expenditures.

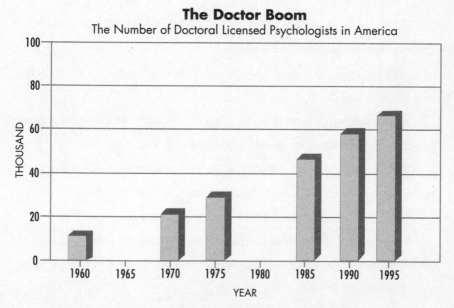

The Doctor Boom
The Number of Doctoral Licensed Psychologists in America

From *Manufacturing Victims*, by Dr. Tana Dineen, Robert Davies Multimedia Publishing, 1996.

Many of these people, I fear, are professional victims, draining resources in their unending search for rescue.

The irony, of course, is that rescue is the problem, not the solution.

Here's my favorite rescue joke. This guy named Joe prays to God to win the lottery, week after week, year in and year out. Never happens. Joe begins to doubt the very existence of God. Finally he cries up to the heavens, "God! Time after time I have prayed to you for this one thing! And you have never answered my prayers. Why, God, why? What more must I do?" A mighty voice booms down. "Joe! Do me a favor! Buy a ticket."

Blame

Imagine that you're in a canoe with a friend and there's a fork in the river. Your friend convinces you to take the channel on the right. Next thing you know, you hear the roar of a waterfall. What do you do?

Do you start yelling at your friend? Of course not! It's counterproductive. You paddle like hell for shore.

Let's say you make it. *Now* do you start screaming? That's what a lot of people would do. But why?

You've paid your tuition—a brush with disaster—so learn the lesson: Blame solves nothing. It's counterproductive. Irrelevant.

Blame is just the flip side of rescue. It's another way of ceding your personal power to somebody else. When you blame someone, you're telling her, "You have control over my feelings and fate, not I."

When you're in the middle of a life-threatening situation, you naturally ignore blame. It's a survival instinct. But life itself is the ultimate life-threatening situation, because all life ends. You are headed for certain death, now and every moment of your life. The same instinct to ignore blame should apply.

But it doesn't. We take the finite, wondrous accident of our own existence for granted and act as if we can play self-destructive blame games forever. We pity ourselves and hate those who have hurt us. We hold grudges, sometimes seek revenge, take secret pleasure in the suffering of those we blame—and feel totally justified.

Worse still, we commonly withhold our love from the people who have helped us the most—our parents—usually because with all that help, there was some hurt, too. We label our parents with terms such as "dysfunctional," "toxic," and "emotionally abusive," and allow these labels to influence not just our feelings, but our very memories, sometimes so much that we begin to rewrite history. Anything outside the label fades in our recollection, to the point where it may as well have never happened. In the name of healing and self-discovery, we ignore the greatest gifts of love we've ever been given.

Some parents really are abusive. But the vast majority are just imperfect people who make about the same number of mistakes parenting as they do in the other aspects of their lives. Even so, the very foundation of modern clinical psychology is grounded upon blaming parents for the problems of their adult children.

When the concept of blaming parents for adult problems was first popularized in the 1950s, it was a valuable addition to understanding human behavior. After all, early parental influence is important. But current research shows that it's not as important as many psychologists still believe. It's just one part of the big picture, along with such other crucial factors as brain biochemistry, adult experiences, hormonal impact, peer influence, and genetic traits. Oh, and let's not forget one other little factor: you. There is a *you* in you that nobody put there.

One of the best examples of exaggerating parental influence is the notion that adult children of alcoholics are uniformly scarred. This idea was so consistent with the conventional wisdom of psychology that it became widely accepted in the 1990s. But now research shows that adult children of alcoholics are as mentally healthy as most people.

Even parents, though, are not at the top of the list of those we blame. Virtually all people have the same favorite target: themselves.

Even people who don't blame others often blame themselves. It feels tough and strong to blame yourself. But it's the opposite.

It's not a sign of strength, but of fear. When you run into difficulties and take the fork in the road that leads to fear, a natural reaction is to blame yourself. Fear needs a bad guy, just as rescue needs a hero.

But when you blame yourself, all you do is reinforce fear. You convince yourself that your worst dread is real: You're not good enough! When you believe this, the wound you create becomes a huge emotional drain. It's as if a psychological artery has been severed, causing you to bleed out, until your personal power has been drained.

Even as this happens, though, many people are still proud of themselves, thinking that they are taking responsibility. Blame isn't responsibility. Responsibility is about using personal power and making changes. Blame is about sabotaging personal power and staying frozen in fear. Responsibility is a call to action; blame is a call to anger. Action solves problems; anger solves nothing. Anger is just fear wearing the mask of aggression.

Because blame is inspired by fear, the strongest force against it is love.

When your heart is focused on love, you don't indulge in blame.

Love comes from the spirit and intellect, which have no interest in blame. The spirit and intellect are innately constructive and shun all destructive impulses, including blame.

And even when blame already exists, love wipes it away. The purest form of love—appreciation—creates compassion for others and for oneself. Blame wilts in the face of this far stronger force.

This approach to quelling blame may sound simple—because it is. But it's only simple to see—hard to do.

I can help you see it. Only you can do it.

But you *can* do it. Your life belongs to you alone, and the future holds all that you need. At your side, enforcing your will upon your own world, you have the powers of perception, of choice, of appreciation, and of intellect.

These forces support your personal power. And this power gives you the chance to stop destroying yourself.

You will never wield this power, however, until you free yourself from the VERBs. The VERBs cripple the personal power you need to seize the happiness you desire. Do these four things, and your life will begin to change.

◆ When you begin to feel like a victim, stop!
◆ When you begin to feel entitled, stop!
◆ When you begin to feel the need for rescue, stop!
◆ When you begin to feel the need to blame, stop!

Turn away from these tools of destruction—and use the happiness tools. This is what happy people do.

CHAPTER SEVEN

The Awful Grace
of God

He had told his daughter he had come to Canyon Ranch to heal. But he had come here to die.

I could see it in his eyes. They were unfocused, scattered, almost shattered with pain, like two glassy marbles that had cracked but somehow remained intact. The human sparkle, that illumination of the soul, was gone from them. There was no light, no life.

He had seen too much of death lately, and it had seeped into his soul and become an almost comforting presence, beckoning him to come rest from his pain. His daughter, who first brought him to my office, was so frightened by it that she had become overtly maternal, as if he were her child.

He felt that he had no real possibilities—no choices whatsoever about the course of his remaining days. His sense of security was gone, love was just another bitter memory, and his life's work lay in ruins.

As I sat down with him for the first time, I wanted to ask him what was still good in his life, what his talents were, what his strengths were, and what still sparked his appreciation. Those were the things that could save him.

But this wasn't the time.

"What brings you here?" I asked.

Between deep, leaden breaths, he told me of his tragedy. Eighteen months earlier, his wife, only in her early sixties, had died painfully from congestive heart failure. They had been deeply in love, and her slow death had left him numb. He had retreated into his work and had begun to find solace. He was extremely successful, an entrepreneur owner of an engineering consulting firm, and many of his 153 employees were like family. His best friends, those who had helped him build the company from the ground up, reached out to him in his sorrow, and together they had shared their mutual memories of his wife. Over long months, he again began to relish his role as the leader of a family of friends who were among the best civil engineers in the world. They built dams, roads, and power plants that would last for centuries. Despite his loss, he realized, he and his colleagues still had enviable lives. They loved their work, were devoted to one another, and enjoyed the perquisites of wealth: penthouse apartments in New York City, summer homes in the Hamptons, classic automobiles, exotic vacations, and a luxurious, eagle's-nest office space near the lofty top of the World Trade Center.

And one morning, all that was still good in his life was gone.

In Frankfurt on business, he watched CNN in frantic revulsion as he lost his friends and colleagues. All of them. All 153. His executive secretary was on her cell phone with him as it occurred, hyperventilating with fear, barely coherent, until their connection abruptly turned into a high electronic whine. He told me that he heard that sound in his sleep now—heard it everywhere.

Before he even made it back home, to attend the first of an overwhelming series of funerals, he was almost broke. His company's assets had consisted primarily of intellectual property, the knowledge that was in the minds of his 153 dead friends. He had a little 401(k) money left, but not much else. He had to put his Manhattan townhouse on the market immediately, and it was the worst possible time to sell.

He missed that money—not the way he missed his wife and his friends, but he missed it. He missed everything, everyone, every day. He was dumbstruck that a life so good could suddenly become such hell.

It was far more than his heart could bear. His blood pressure rocketed so high over the next month that it caused his ears to ring with tinnitus—that whine! Inescapable! Despite being on medication, he had an ischemic stroke.

The stroke left him with moderate hemiparesis, causing his right foot to drag and his speech to slur. Only months before, he'd been a Central Park weekend warrior and a mountain climber—and now this. A cripple. His slurred speech gave the false impression of permanent mental debility. Even his own body had betrayed him.

The assault of sorrow shook his spirit. He was irritable and mentally detached, and every little upset—even something as trivial as my phone ringing during our session—was channeled straight into his fear system. His fear-storing amygdala seemed to be in overdrive, and his endocrine glands had saddled him with the characteristics of a hot reactor.

His real-world trauma and his ingrained fears had begun to merge, leaving him unable to distinguish realistic fear from paranoia. In the dance of the spirit and reptile, his reptile was definitely leading.

Not being able to control his fear was horrible for him; it made him feel like a big baby. But that was just one of many weaknesses he'd discovered in himself since his troubles had begun. Without the support of his wife, friends, and finances, he'd found that he was more shy and reserved than he'd thought, that he was a control freak and an unrealistic perfectionist, and that he was overly sensitive to slights. There's nothing like having your world ripped apart to expose all your flaws.

Thus, on top of everything else, he was starting to hate himself. He was ashamed of his weaknesses and feared that they would sabotage any effort at recovery.

To escape this horror, he had aimed himself straight at self-destruction. He was drinking heavily, mixing sedatives with alcohol, hardly bothering to eat, chain smoking, and sitting around most of the day in a funk of booze and smoke. At the rate he was going, another stroke seemed inevitable.

But why was he here? He could have checked in to a hotel to die. Something in him wanted to live, and I had to find it. Fast.

Through tears and frequent shudders, he told me his story. After no more than 30 or 40 minutes, I began to lead him away from his catharsis. He could have stayed there forever, railing against fate until another blood vessel blew up in his brain, but we had work to do.

"Did you get counseling at home?" I asked.

"Yeah. A Park Avenue psychiatrist told me he could cure me, if I'd commit to at least 26 sessions."

"Cure you of what?"

"Depression."

"Depression? You'd be crazy not to be depressed."

Involuntarily, he started to smile, but smiling didn't seem to fit his face anymore.

"Let's do something," I said. "Tell me one of your best memories of your wife."

"I don't think I . . ."

"I know," I said gently. "Do it anyway."

He tiptoed into the subject, shied away, went back, gained momentum, and soon was lost in it, reliving a happy moment when she'd met him for a picnic at the base camp of a mountain in Nepal, where cobalt skies were burned by a huge yellow sun. He pulled a wrinkled photo out of his wallet, and there she was, in Nepal, beautiful big eyes burning with life. As he kept talking, the photo still in his hand, his energy expanded, unfolding like a morning glory at dawn.

I interrupted him. "Right this second, how do you feel?"

He looked puzzled, quizzical. "Alive?" He said it as if it were a word in a half-forgotten language—a word he didn't want to remember.

Building Strengths

The reason the Park Avenue psychiatrist had wanted to schedule 26 sessions, I'm sure, is because it takes at least that long to make a dent in someone's problems and weaknesses. Unfortunately, though, a dent is about all you can ever make when you go to war against problems and weaknesses.

Face facts: How can someone "come to closure" over losing his wife, his friends, his fortune, and his health?

My new client was nothing less than a latter-day Job—a proud man ground to dust—and that's how I came to think of him, as Job. Could you sit in a room with a man like Job and tell him you could fix his problems? Not even a doctorate in cynical psychology prepares you for that.

With all that had happened, there was only one way for Job to have a last chance at happiness: building on his strengths.

Job needed to make one of the most important perceptual shifts that exists: shifting his focus from his problems and weaknesses to his possibilities and strengths. This would be the hardest thing he'd ever done.

But the alternative was suffering and death—first spiritual, then biological. If he stayed fixated on his problems and weaknesses, he would wander forever down the dark road of fear. On that road, he'd meet many more weaknesses, create new problems, indulge in the VERBs, do the Dirty Ds, and travel in circles until all life had left him.

On the other hand, if he had the courage to take the other fork in the road, the one that led to the neocortical powers of his spirit and intellect, he had a shot at redemption. On that road, he could begin a cycle of healing. If he did, though, he would be vulnerable to loss again. It would be a tough choice for him.

But it would be a choice, and I was hoping that the empowering act of making a choice would revitalize him, at least enough to awaken his appreciation of what he still had left in his life. If this happened, the magical force of appreciation would lend energy to his personal power and give him one last chance.

Some psychologists, I'm sure, would look at a desperate case like this and say, "Wow, this guy is finished! Fixing him would be like trying to make something out of nothing! That's alchemy—and it's impossible!"

But to say that would be to assume that at the core of every human being there is . . . nothing. It would be to assume that all you are is the sum product of the nurture and the nature of your parents, plus the influence of society.

But, as I've said, there is a *you* in you that nobody put there. It will always be there, no matter how terrible the tragedies that try to snuff it out. Call it the soul, call it the divine spirit, call it the ego, call it whatever you want. It's there. I know it's there, because I've met too many people who were busted down to nothing—*nothing!*—who still had it.

Job still had it, but it was going to take a powerful perceptual shift for him to get much good out of it. He needed to look past his loss and see what was on the other side of sorrow. If he kept looking into his deep well of loss, he might be able to hold back his pain, but pain would be all he'd ever again see. He'd never be happy.

To use a mathematical analogy, solving all your problems might take you from a negative ten to zero—but it doesn't automatically take you to a plus ten. You're still stuck at zero, and who wants to settle for that? Happy people don't. Furthermore, when you focus on problems, it's hard even to get to zero, because you become bogged down in your own negativity and fear. It's much smarter to focus on possibilities and leapfrog past zero without even stopping.

However, several of the most powerful institutions in our society strongly orient us toward weaknesses and problems. The institution of modern medicine, for one, is focused excessively on fighting disease instead of building health. That was appropriate in the early 20th century, when the primary health threats were the communicable disease epidemics, such as smallpox and typhoid; but now, when the primary health threats are degenerative diseases, it's inappropriate.

Unfortunately, the institution of clinical psychology patterned itself

What Happy People Know

after modern medicine and now focuses excessively on psychological pathologies, instead of concentrating on, as Dr. Martin Seligman puts it, the "sanities," such as courage and optimism. Stark evidence of this: At recent count, there had been 54,040 professional articles written on depression and 415 on happiness.

Another powerful institution, the news media, is also notoriously pinpointed upon problems, because that's where the action is. Once I asked a network CEO why he never ran any good-news shows, and he said, "Because they don't sell."

Furthermore, the insurance industry, of course, is also fixated upon problems. Can you imagine a psychologist trying to get third-party payment for his client's work on wisdom?

And the advertising and marketing industries, needless to say, are dedicated to making you think you have all kinds of problems that only their products can fix.

We live in a sea of negativity. Sometimes I'm amazed that positive medical psychology even exists. But it does, and I was certain it was the only approach that had even a chance of saving Job's life.

The Worst of It

To help me find Job's strengths, the second time I saw him I began to do constructive questioning. I didn't just probe his problems and rake open his wounds, all in the name of insight. Instead, I searched his psyche for solutions. These solutions would be the positive possibilities that would help him zoom past zero and achieve happiness.

Standard psychotherapeutic questions would just make him more depressed, defensive, and pessimistic, since they're all just variations of

"What's wrong with you?" They would be good for catharsis, but more catharsis wouldn't help Job. He could rant and rave all day long, but when he was done, his problems would still be there, and his amygdala would still be full of fear.

"When were you the happiest in your life?" I asked Job.

He thought about it. "When I first got married," he said, without much conviction.

"What did you like about being a newlywed?"

"My wife, I guess."

"What would you say is your greatest strength at this point in your life?"

"To be honest," he said—but it didn't sound like that; with his slurring it came out, T'b on-us—"I don't feel like I have any strengths left."

"When in your life did you feel strongest?"

"After the birth of . . ." He stopped abruptly.

"Your daughter?"

He shook his head.

"Who?"

He shook his head again.

Very slowly, he said, "I didn't tell you everything yesterday." His words came hard, as if talking were torture.

"What didn't you tell me?" I had a sense of dread.

"The worst of it."

I didn't say anything. No big strategy. I just didn't want to hear it.

"I have a son." His voice caught, choked. "He worked with me." Tears were dropping onto his shirt. "In my office. I had a son."

"Oh, my God."

He looked into my eyes, and nodded yes to the question I was afraid to ask.

I sat there like a bump on a log. I don't know how long. I didn't know what to say.

Finally, "I lost a son, too."

"You did?"

I'd like to tell you that I reached out to him, but that wasn't the way it happened. He reached out to me, and we embraced.

I could feel his compassion. I hope that he felt mine. At that moment, we were brothers, in the brotherhood of the walking wounded. It's not unusual for me to feel a kinship of suffering with the people I meet. People don't come to me with good news.

We are all walking wounded.

In our own way, with our own losses, we are all Job.

And yet, despite our suffering, we stay so strong! It's astonishing how strong most people are. With death inevitable and pain a part of every day, we still wake up each morning with new plans, and sleep each night with new dreams.

We build a better world each workday of our lives, without the slightest hope of being alive in 100 years to reap the reward. We say that we're doing it for our children, or for our children's children, but the childless among us do it, too—because building is simply what people do.

Why do we do it? That's easy: because it feels good.

This good feeling is critical to our survival. Feeling good, most people think, is an end unto itself, a final destination. But emotions are never just destinations. They are the beginnings of our activities as much as they are the results of them. This is easy to understand when you consider negative emotions. Fear and anger, obviously, are feelings that usually trigger the activities of fighting, fleeing, or freezing. By the same token, positive emotions also trigger activities—positive activities, such as building. These positive activities are just as important to our survival as negative activities.

Happiness researcher Dr. Barbara Frederickson has noted that joy is probably the single most powerful trigger of exploration and creativity, and that love is by far the strongest force in creating human bonding and cooperation.

These activities, in turn, profoundly affect the body's brain chemistry and endocrine function. They increase production of the feel-good neurotransmitter dopamine and create calm, strong cardiovascular function. These physical effects then reinforce the original positive feeling, in an upward spiral of good feeling and good function.

Upward spirals, Dr. Frederickson has shown in studies, enable people to solve their own problems. Positive spirals increase people's ability to come up with a broad variety of creative options, and to put these options into action. Dr. Frederickson calls this "the broaden and build theory of positive emotions."

Resting at the core of this theory is the virtually irrefutable fact that it feels good to exercise your own strongest powers. Always has, always will. Your capacity for this enjoyment is hardwired into your brain.

This hardwiring starts early in life. About 2 months prior to birth, the fetal brain begins to make connections among its 100 billion brain cells. Neurons develop branchlike dendrites that touch other neurons, creating the connections that lead to thought. By about age 3, practically every cell in the brain has made connections with other cells. There are a staggering number of these connections.

In fact, there are more connections than the brain can handle. So much information flies from connection to connection that it's overwhelming. This contributes to the distractible, scattered state of mind that is common among babies and toddlers. Their consciousness is, in effect, a mile wide and an inch deep. If development were to continue in this manner, the brain would soon lose its ability to focus, and mental function would degenerate to that of a person with autism or certain types of schizophrenia.

Therefore, the brain, at about age 3, begins to make a critical shift. It starts to ignore many connections. It neglects the connections that don't work very well, that are difficult to exercise, or that hold little innate interest. When this happens, these connections grow weaker. They become rather like footpaths that have been allowed to fall into disrepair. Deprived of the brain chemicals that keep them healthy, they begin to die.

As these connections die, the brain shifts its biochemical support system to the connections that work well and hold the most interest. These healthy, interesting connections get even stronger. They begin to take advantage of a learning phenomenon that favors frequently used connections. This phenomenon (called long-term potentiation), dictates that each time a connection is used, it becomes even easier to use. This accounts for the fact that if you review the same information five times, you aren't five times more likely to remember it, but about 20 times more likely.

This shift of energy from the weak connections to the strong ones continues until the late teenage years. By that time, almost half of the connections that you had at age 3 are gone. They're dead, and it's virtually impossible to revive them. But the neural connections that are still alive are stronger than ever. Talent is born! When this talent is exercised again and again, it becomes a strength. This strength becomes an integral part of you—one of the best parts.

Strengths are tremendously divergent. They can be anything from being good at math, to being good with horses, to being good with people.

As people realize their strengths, they generally take advantage of them. They do it for the same basic reason that a toddler develops strengths in the first place: because it feels good.

Many people turn their strengths into careers. That's smart. It gives them not only a competitive edge but, more important, the joy and passion that inspire success.

Many other people, though, make the mistake of not following their strengths, but following money. Ironically, they often end up unsuccessful, because they don't love their work and aren't necessarily talented at it.

When people do follow their strengths, and use them every day, they become increasingly intelligent. Within their brains, a wondrous thing happens: the creation of the *ultimate brain cell*.

These ultimate brain cells start out at birth as normal brain cells. Over time, though, as the cells make connections again and again, they begin to grow. They don't get bigger in size as they grow, but instead send out increasing branches of dendrites to connect with other cells. At the very beginning of a brain cell's life, it may have only one dendritic branch. But if it is biochemically nourished through the phenomenon of long-term potentiation, it grows new dendrites, branching off the sides of existing dendrites.

This takes many years. Over the course of a lifetime, a dendrite might send out four, five, or even six branches.

The first five branches are basically identical. But the sixth branch, or side, is remarkable. Unlike the first five, it has the amazing ability to keep growing. It can explore and seek out new connections on its own. When this occurs, it creates the ultimate brain cell, capable of finding knowledge that is out of the reach of lesser cells.

Often, this knowledge is not straightforward factual knowledge, such as one plus one equals two. Ordinary brain cells can figure that out. Instead, it is knowledge about the meaning, significance, and connection of facts. It is the highest form of knowledge: wisdom. Wisdom almost always ushers in happiness, and was recently shown by Walter Bortz, M.D., of Stanford University, to be the best single predictor for aging well.

The existence of these ultimate brain cells was discovered quite recently by eminent neurologist Dr. Marian Diamond. Dr. Diamond expresses her discovery like this: "We began with a nerve cell, which starts in the embryo as just a sort of sphere. It sends its first branch out to overcome ignorance. As it reaches out, it is gathering knowledge and it is becoming creative. Then we become a little more idealistic, generous, and altruistic. But it is our six-sided dendrites which give us wisdom."

Wisdom, however, never develops in a vacuum. To grow, a sixth-branch dendrite must be actively searching for knowledge. In this search, it is partly motivated by the pleasure of using strong neuronal connections. But at this mature stage of brain development, which generally occurs in midlife or later, pleasure alone is not always enough to prompt the search. Often, the motivation for growth, at this elevated level of consciousness, is to understand suffering—in hopes of ending it.

This is not the type of motivation anyone wants. But it is often the most compelling motivation that life offers.

This can be perceived as tragic. Or beautiful.

After all, is it not beautiful that suffering can create wisdom? What if suffering created only . . . suffering? *That* would be tragic.

The Greek dramatist Aeschylus commented poetically upon this more than 2,500 years ago, when he wrote the following.

He who learns must suffer.
Even in our sleep,
Pain which we cannot forget
Falls drop by drop upon the heart,
Until, in our own despair,
Against our will,
Comes wisdom,
Through the awful grace of God.

Wisdom—coming *against* our will: There is no finer description of the true nature of optimism. People usually think that optimism is created by things going well, but as I've mentioned, that only creates complacency. Optimism comes from pain—from finally realizing that the more painful the event, the more powerful the lesson. When you finally figure out that what hurts you the most teaches you the most, then you have a shield against suffering—the shield of optimism. You know that nothing is all bad.

My client Job was suffering as much as any person I'd ever met. His pain was bad enough to kill most people, and I knew it would kill him, too, if he kept walking down the fork in the road that leads only to fear.

But he was a wise man, certain to have an abundance of six-branch neurons. I knew he had many strengths. After a week of seeing him every day, I felt that I had discovered the strengths that could save him.

The Suffering of Job

Philosopher Friedrich Nietzsche said of suffering, "That which doesn't kill me makes me stronger." For the past 100 years, people have repeated this aphorism.

God knows why. It's stupid.

Suffering that doesn't kill you *might* make you stronger—or it might pound you right into the ground, weak and beaten, still alive but wishing you weren't. It all depends on how you respond to it.

If you respond primarily with your fear system, suffering will make you weaker. You'll fixate on your faults, begin to feel helpless, do the Dirty Ds to yourself, get caught up in the VERBs—and fade away.

However, if you respond with the neocortical powers of your spirit and intellect, you'll have a chance to learn optimism, find meaning in your pain, become proactive—and achieve wisdom. But none of this will be possible unless you lead with your strengths. You can't overcome suffering with anything less than your best.

I felt that I had found the best in Job. But he had to find it, too. I couldn't heal him. Only he could do that. So the next time I saw him, I started by asking more constructive questions.

"What was your company worth at its peak?" I asked. "Approximately."

"Approximately $25 to $35 million, based on our earnings."

"And how much of that was yours?"

"Lion's share."

"Ever think about selling?"

"Never seriously."

"How come?"

"I loved it. Loved the work. To me, there's nothing like being an engineer and making something out of nothing. And I loved the organizing, the managing. Mostly, though, I loved the people." He took a deep breath. "Loved working with my son."

"What would have happened to your employees if you'd sold the company?"

"With new management, a lot of them would have fallen by the wayside. That was part of the reason I could never sell."

"You really care about people."

"Doesn't everybody?"

I shook my head. "You'd be amazed."

I asked him to tell me about his favorite employee. His face lit up. He started talking about a tough old seat-of-the-pants engineer who'd been his mentor way back when, in a small company in the Texas Panhandle. As he talked about old times, his memories became so vivid that they were almost like flashbacks. That's the power of appreciation! It can cut through time like a knife, cut through pain, cut through almost anything, to the point where only love is left, and all the rest is meaningless.

"Was he there?" I asked.

"On the 11th?" He nodded slowly, and his eyes started to float in tears, but happiness was still on his face, bittersweet now, as happiness so often is.

"Here's something important," I said. We locked eyes. "However much you're hurting right now, it's equal to the love that's left in you."

He looked surprised, doubtful, as if surely all love had deserted him when those he loved had died. But the common sense of it hit home and resonated with his wisdom, and I could tell he knew it was true.

"Then I must have a lot of love left." He said it with great sadness, but not a trace of self-pity.

"You must."

He sat quietly, letting it sink in.

"What do you think your single greatest strength is?" I asked.

"I care about people," he said, as if stating the obvious.

"What's your second greatest strength?"

"I'm a hell of an engineer."

Bingo! I'd been right. "I agree. Completely. Those are your two greatest strengths. So what are you going to do with them?"

He answered so quickly that I knew he'd been thinking about it. "Re-engineer my life. Around other people."

"How so?"

"I'm going to start a foundation." His voice was strong, full of conviction. "For the survivors of 9/11. I'll hire my daughter to help."

Spontaneously, I gave him a high five. That's not something I normally do. It's kid stuff. But at that moment, I felt like a kid. Young. Strong. Good at what I do.

Back from the Brink

But how do you start a foundation?

According to Job, who had already been working with his daughter on it by the next time we met, you do it the same way you start an engineering firm. I bowed to his expertise. He was a man of great accomplishment.

I hope I've never given you the impression in this book that the guests at Canyon Ranch lack emotional intelligence. Despite their problems, most of them are wise, energetic, and creative, and often the best thing I can do is just help them tap their own inner wisdom.

That applies to most people. The people I've counseled have almost all been eager to feel better, and have taught me as much as I've taught them. After all, this book isn't called *What I Know about Happiness (and You Don't)*. I know that means I'm not the Great Dr. Painbuster, but that's been a phony role since the day it was concocted. You're the hero of your own story.

Just as Job was the hero of his. The new story of his life that he had begun to tell was "Back from the Brink," and he was gaining momentum with it every day. He wasn't becoming something new, but was becoming his old self. Being a victim just didn't fit him.

One thing I was able to introduce to Job, though, was the concept called Best Practices. Best Practices is a tool for building better businesses that I learned from corporate consultants David Cooperrider and Diana Whitney, who also created the Appreciative Inquiry concept.

At first, I applied the concept strictly to businesses. I soon discovered, though, that the Best Practices technique is as effective for individuals as it is for organizations.

In organizations, such as the one Job was starting, the concept consists of identifying the existing practices that are the most efficient, the most profitable—the most conducive to success. It doesn't focus at all on solving problems, but often solves them anyway, by leapfrogging past zero to positive territory.

Businesses, in a sense, work like brains, with each employee, in effect, acting as a single brain cell. Like many of the neuronal connections in brains, the connections among employees are often established for the sole purpose of solving problems. Thus, businesses are hardwired for hard times. Because of this, that's sometimes all a company can see—its problems and weaknesses, instead of its possibilities and strengths.

Best Practices helps businesses focus on what they do best. Companies don't last when they try to do all things adequately, at the expense of excellence in their strongest areas.

Groups of employees, like groups of neuronal connections, thrive when they're allowed to do what they do best. It gives them energy. When they have to spend their time troubleshooting, putting out fires, and fixing problems, they tend to become exhausted, unhappy, and inefficient.

Individuals, running their own lives, are the same way. They get energy from building on their successes, not fighting their failures.

Almost every time I counsel guests at the Ranch, I ask them to identify their Best Personal Practices, using constructive questions like these.

- What makes you happiest?
- When were you happiest?
- How did you become happy then?
- What do you like most about yourself?
- What creates that quality?
- How do you make that quality last?
- When did you have that quality the most?
- How could you create more of it?
- What gives you peace of mind?
- What brings out the best in you?
- Who appreciates you the most? Why?
- What are your primary strengths?
- What are your core beliefs?
- What values do you live by?
- Who is in your emotional support network?
- What best helps you feel creative?

I could go on and on. There are hundreds of questions that help people figure out the things that make their lives work.

One of the advantages of Best Personal Practices is that it helps people distinguish their strengths from their dreams. Dreams are fine, but too many people confuse what they *wish* they were good at with what they really are good at. They live in a dream world.

All our lives we're told, You can do anything you set your mind to! But you can't. If that were true, we'd all be movie stars, pro athletes, and presidents. Personally, I'd be this year's Super Bowl MVP.

This form of self-delusion was launched as a major crusade in psychology in the 1950s, with the advent of the power-of-positive-thinking movement. It was a good idea, but some people now take positive thinking all the way to la-la land. They say things like, "You create your own reality." Sorry. Not on this planet. You create your own perception and your own meaning, but reality is reality.

I'd never have had the nerve to tell Job that he had created his reality, and that now he could create a new, improved one. The only thing he and I talked about was making the best of what he actually had.

By the end of his third week at the Ranch, he'd already rented a New York office, sight unseen, that would be the incubator for his new foundation. He had gotten pledges for more than $100,000. He was pumped. Still grieving, of course. That was part of his life now. The point was, he *had* a life again.

The last time I had a session with him, he did a lot more talking than I did. The change in him was remarkable. Even his physical symptoms—the slurring of his speech and the weakness in his foot—had improved immeasurably. Credit for the improvement went partly to the Ranch's excellent rehabilitation staff, but mostly to Job himself, who had soared past his weaknesses by summoning his strengths. When human beings decide to take back their power, it's hard to hold them down.

As he told me his plans for the future, one of the last things he said was, "You know how they say that nobody on his deathbed ever wishes he'd spent more time at the office?"

"I do."

"That's really a load of crap, isn't it? I love the office."

I gave him another high five. I couldn't help myself.

Job's Daughter

She stuck her head in the door as I was saying good-bye to Job and said, "Knock-knock."

"Come on in," Job said, as if the office were his own. "I'm giving Dan our new fax number and e-mail and all that."

She looked radiant. Her blue eyes were burning with life, as her mother's had, long ago, in Nepal.

"I wanted to say thanks," she said to me. She held out her hand.

"You're saying it to the wrong guy."

She looked at her father, gave him a little smile, and at first it was just an ordinary kind of look, but he held her gaze, looked deeply within her, and it turned into something very important between them. A family thing.

With unutterable sadness, he said, "I'm so sorry."

She fell into his chest, and he was her father again, he was back, caring for his family, doing what he did best, and they both began to weep, but there seemed to be no sadness left in the weeping, just relief, and love.

"Oh, Daddy."

I left the room, as quietly as I could.

CHAPTER EIGHT

The Story of My Life

G et on in here now," the man in shiny dress slacks and a dirty plaid shirt said to his daughter. He took her by the wrist and pulled her across the threshold of my office, a real-life Raggedy Ann. Her eyes pinballed around the room, as if she were looking everywhere and nowhere at the same time. Mom followed meekly behind.

Dad sat in a chair and tugged his daughter's wrist until she plopped into the one beside it. Mom stood, hanging back, motionless as a picture on the wall. He pulled out a pack of Camels and lit one without consulting anybody, a relatively common practice in the early 1970s, even in a medical office like this one at the University of Nebraska, near a state school for the deaf.

In sign language, I said to the 9-year-old girl, "Hello, Ally." But she looked right through me.

"Little Ally-Cat don't know hand signs," said her father.

"Now she does know a few," Mom offered quietly. "I taught her ones for hungry, and potty, and water and such."

Dad grimaced and looked for a place to drop his ash. He settled for his palm, rubbed it in a little, and let the remainder fall to the floor. "Ya ask me," he said, "there ain't no way, no how, nuthin's gonna come from this."

Wow! A quadruple negative! Did that add up to a positive? Probably not, coming from this guy's mouth. He was what we rural Midwesterners used to call a "poor dirt farmer"—an angry man about six steps out of the Stone Age.

Looking at a guy like that, you wanted to blame his background, but the fact was, his older brother—a product of the same background—had worked his way up to being manager and part owner of a local farm implement distributorship. As I've mentioned, there's a *you* in you that nobody put there, and it can give you a good life, if you choose to let it. But this man, it seemed to me, had stopped making choices a long time ago, probably after he'd hit some snags. Now he was just reacting to various problems as they arose and calling it life.

Ally, short for Alison, had come to the School for the Deaf, a live-in facility not far from a medical school, because she was getting no special ed—which meant no education at all—back home, deep in the humid hinterlands of corn country. She was capable of only primitive communication—basic point-and-grunt—and her behavior was crude and wild.

Her parents hadn't realized that she was profoundly deaf until she was 3, because hearing wasn't routinely checked at birth back then. But by age 3, she had already retreated into her small world of playing with the farm animals and wandering down to a gully to play by herself, while her mom worked in the vegetable patch.

"Dr. Baker," said the wife, whose name was Rita, "do you think you can teach Ally to talk? 'Cuz I saw this TV show on it, where they did that. I'd love to know what's goin' on in that little head a hers." She looked at Ally with genuine affection and terrible sadness. All these years—and they'd never talked.

"I think so," I said. And I meant it. But the lead pediatrician at the med school had been less hopeful. He had described Ally as a "feral child," the human equivalent of a wild animal, and had said it was extremely difficult to introduce language to kids as old as she. You could teach them palpable, material concepts, he said, like "food" and "bed," but abstractions were tough.

"When she does learn to talk," I said, "it will probably be with sign language."

"Story a my life," Rita sighed. "My little girl finally learns to talk, and it's a language me and Pa will never know."

That was one way to look at it, I guess.

"You could learn to sign," I said.

"She don't have time." Her husband glared at her and saved a little for me.

I could have tangled with Pa over that, but I was too young and dumb (and scared). He was big, and he used his bulk to intimidate. Besides, as a fledgling psychologist, I'd been trained to change how people thought, not how they lived. Those were two different things. That was the thinking back then, believe it or not.

Ally, squirming fitfully, grabbed a water pitcher on my desk and started to fill my glass with it. I watched intently, because I'd been reviewing research by famed child psychologist Jean Claude Piaget, who charted the stages of development. If he was right, a developmentally delayed child like Ally would be stuck in her "preoperational" phase, in which she could not comprehend that the glass could hold only so much water. The concept would be too abstract.

Sure enough—splash! Water all over the desk.

Ally's dad slapped at her hands and cursed, and she ran over to her mom and burrowed in. "Sorry 'bout that," said Rita, but I wasn't paying much attention. I was off in theory-land.

Theoretically, according to what I had been reading about language-deprived children, Ally was missing more than just a way to communicate. She was missing a way to make sense of the world and manage her own emotions.

The contemporary thinking on language is that it has a magically powerful effect upon the brain. We think in words—and if we don't have words, thinking becomes terribly compromised. Without words, thoughts are just chains of flashing images. They lack structure and cohesion, and they don't have a strong sense of past, present, or future. They often don't even reflect the laws of cause and effect.

When thinking is compromised, emotions become dictators. They overpower logic and run rampant. This further weakens the power of the intellect, in a downward spiral of cognitive decline.

Thus, the brain does not just create language—language also creates the brain. A child's exposure to language has a tremendous impact upon his or her eventual level of cognitive ability. This impact begins even before birth. One study, for example, showed that 4-day-old Russian babies responded more actively to the Russian language, which they had heard in utero, than they did to a foreign language. Another revealing study proving the monumental impact of language charted the average number of words 42 children heard each day during the first 2½ years of their lives. The kids of the most articulate parents heard an average of 2,100 words every hour. The kids of moderately articulate parents heard an average of 1,200 words per hour. The children of inarticulate parents heard only 600 words per hour. When all the children were tested at age 3 for intelligence, those who'd heard the most words did by far the best—and continued to do the best throughout grade school.

Most fascinating of all, the kids who heard the most words also heard the most constructive words—words of encouragement, hope, empowerment, and love. The kids who didn't hear many words, the researchers noted, heard a disproportionate number of destructive words: "Stop that!" "That's too loud!" and "Go away!"

The quality of the words made a profound impact upon emotional development. The kids who were exposed to the most constructive language excelled at bonding, good behavior, and self-esteem. The other kids didn't. This was not because the other kids had significantly harder lives than the kids of articulate parents. The kids who heard negative language were also loved by their parents, and there was no evidence of any significant abuse against any of the children. Furthermore, all three groups of children faced approximately the same number of serious traumas, including divorces among parents, illnesses, and the deaths of loved ones.

The biggest difference in their lives was simply the language they were reared with. The kids who heard the most positive language tended to view the world in the most positive terms.

Even so, it's tempting to look at this study and reduce the role of language to that of mere messenger: It wasn't the loving words that helped, some might say; it was the love. Of course, love is important, but without words to define and memorialize it, even love can be forgettable and nebulous, like the shape of a cloud that can look like anything or nothing until someone names it.

After all, it was clear to me that Rita loved Ally, but even this powerful emotion would never have its full force and effect upon Ally until the day she could finally understand the words "I love you." And say them.

Author Joseph Jaworski has stated this view of the importance of language with great eloquence in his book *Synchronicity: The Inner Path of Leadership*. He has written, "As I considered the importance of language and how human beings interact with the world, it struck me that in many ways the development of language was like the discovery of fire. It was such an incredible primordial force. I had always thought we used language to describe the world. Now I was seeing that was not the case. To the contrary, it is through language that we create the world, because it's nothing until we describe it. And when we describe it, we create distinctions that govern our actions. To put it another way, we do not describe the world we see, *we see the world we describe*."

We see the world we describe! What a revolutionary concept!

What if, then, Ally—a veritable blank slate—were to learn a language that described a world full of beauty and love and personal power? What then?

Then, if the theoreticians were correct, Ally would begin to alchemize these words into thoughts, these thoughts into actions, and these actions into a new life. It could happen—I was certain. Unless someone sabotaged it.

It was hard watching Ally say good-bye to her mother. Rita looked stricken, and Ally was scared. Her little birdlike hands trembled.

It was harder, though, to watch her say good-bye to her dad. He just patted her head and took off. His boots pounded down the hall.

We were alone. Ally looked at me with a sweet smile, her head flocked with blond curls, and reached up toward my face, as if to touch it. I bent down to her and returned her smile. Our eyes met for the first time.

Then she grabbed my glasses and hurled them against the wall so hard they exploded.

I didn't lose my temper—it was just a pair of glasses—and I didn't even speak out loud. But I did mouth the word "Damn."

The second I said it, she ducked into a boxer's crouch, hid her head behind her forearms, and clenched her teeth.

Well, it looked as if Ally did know at least one word.

A Force against Fear

Your capacity for language, like your capacity for fear, is hardwired into your brain. These two capacities have become, through cultural and biological evolution, opposites of one another. Fear is your most deep-seated, primal emotion, and language is the single most fundamental force of your intellect. You have directly experienced their opposition every time in your life that you've tried to talk yourself out of being afraid.

Fear is more deeply embedded, because it resides in the reptilian brain as well as the mammalian brain, but language—which resides in the powerful neocortex—can be stronger than fear.

One of the first uses of language was to serve as a shield against fear and a warning against danger. Even animals have a language of warning. The vervet monkey, for example, can warn other monkeys of an approaching leopard with an alarm call, thus endowing the monkeys with not just protection, but also a greater sense of security.

Animals, in fact, have a larger capacity for language than many people realize. Note the chart below, "Number of Communication Units of Various Species," which indicates the number of separate communication units, or "words," of various species. You probably weren't aware of it, but your guppy knows 15 "words." If you don't believe me, ask him.

However, talking to your guppy can be frustrating, even if you speak

NUMBER OF COMMUNICATION UNITS
OF VARIOUS SPECIES

Fish		Birds		Mammals	
Bullhead:	10	–		–	
Stickleback:	11	–		–	
Guppy:	15	Sparrow:	15	–	
Sunfish:	15	–		*Night monkey:	16
–		–		Deer mouse:	16
–		Great tit:	17	Coati:	17
–		Kingbird:	18	Prairie dog:	18
–		Skua:	18	–	
–		Mallard:	19	–	
Mouthbreeder:	21	Sparrow:	21	Sifaka:	21
–		–		Zebra:	23
–		–		*Patas monkey:	24
–		Chaffinch:	25	Grant's gazelle:	25
–		Coot:	25	Polecat:	25
Badis:	26	Green heron:	26	Elk:	26
–		–		*Dusky titi:	27
–		Hooded gull:	28	–	
–		–		*Tamarin:	32
–		–		*Ring-tailed lemur:	34
–		–		*Rhesus monkey:	37
–		–		*Human being:	45,000–60,000

*Indicates primates
Data from Wilson (1972)

Guppish, because no animal alive can put together a real sentence, despite myths in the popular press. In reality, the most intelligent animals can only learn to sign isolated words, with a few modifiers. Even the most famous "talking animal," the gorilla named Koko, never went beyond simple phrases such as "Go bed" or "Red berry."

Without sign language, taught by humans, animal communication is even more limited. A rhesus monkey, for example, can make 37 different sounds, but each sound is a complete word. Humans can make only about the same number of sounds—44, to be exact—but we can string them together symbolically to create vast numbers of words.

This ability for symbolism, or abstraction, is the single biggest intellectual difference between humans and animals. People know not only what things are, but what they mean. This ability to create meaning, through the complex modifiers of language, gives people the incredible capability of, among other things, finding happiness in ordinary events, and even in misfortune. For example, if a man and a dog both emerged from a terrible car wreck with just scratches, the dog would probably just yelp about the scratches, while the human might feel elated.

The enlightening power of language may have even *created* the unsurpassed intellectual function of the human brain. The fossil record shows that about $3\frac{1}{2}$ million years ago, our ancestors walked upright and looked like humans, but had brains only as large as those of apes. For almost two million years, this brain size stayed approximately the same, and was even smaller than that of the now-extinct Neanderthals. During this time, there was very little evidence of an evolving culture. In one Chinese cave dwelling, for example, people lived for about a half million years—60 times the length of recorded history—huddling over the same fire pits and eating half-cooked bats, with no trace of progress.

However, more than a million years ago, humans began to use a primitive, first-step protolanguage—and shortly after that, their brains began to grow! The human brain went on a 500,000-year growth spurt that resulted in modern-size brains, of about 1,500 to 2,000 cubic centimeters.

Thus, many paleontologists now believe that it wasn't our big human brains that created language, it was language that created our big human brains. Even paleontologists who won't go quite this far still acknowledge that language and intellect are inextricably linked.

Strictly in terms of anatomy, language and higher thought are interwoven. Although language functions are spread throughout the brain, the most active center for language (and particularly for thinking in words) is the left inferior frontal cortex. This area is directly adjacent to, and closely connected to, the left anterior prefrontal cortex, which performs many of the highest thought processes.

These advanced thought processes enable people to experience frightening or upsetting events without reacting automatically with the fear response. This was discovered long ago, in 1840, in the famous case of Phineas Gage, a railroad foreman who survived having a large spike driven into his left anterior prefrontal cortex. Gage was able to function adequately after the accident and could still speak, but had almost no ability to manage his negative emotions.

On occasion, you have probably experienced something somewhat similar to Phineas Gage's predicament. When your neocortical powers have been significantly diminished—due to exhaustion or very low blood sugar—you have probably had a hard time talking yourself out of angry outbursts or fearful thoughts. You may have felt that you just couldn't think straight—that your thoughts were a jumble of emotions and images.

At these times, you probably used the power of language to subdue your confusion, and find meaning in your situation. You probably began to talk to yourself—maybe out loud. Nothing beats words for awakening the neocortex, putting a problem into perspective, and finding possibilities in it.

But when you do this, you face an important choice: what words?

Ally and the Monsters

I saw Ally almost every day. My job was to help kids with developmental disabilities grow emotionally, while the classroom teachers helped them to develop academically.

Her work in class was astonishing. Even though she was 9, which was old for learning a first language, she soaked up words like a sponge. In her first few months of living at the school, she mastered hundreds of nouns and verbs and was making progress with modifiers, syntax, and grammar. Every time she learned a new word from me or her teacher, she would light up with satisfaction, as another piece of her world fit into the cognitive puzzle she was putting together.

Even kids with obstacles as big as Ally's, I have learned, have an intrinsic skill for language. For example, in one study, researchers found that four unrelated deaf children in America and four others in China taught themselves rich vocabularies of over 10,000 different signs, with no training or help. Interestingly, all eight kids invented the same basic gestures, instead of using gestures that reflected their own native languages. This is further evidence, I believe, that language is a multifunctional, inborn ability—like crawling—and not just a skill we learn in order to communicate.

Ally's emotional development, however, went more slowly. In the beginning, she lagged far behind her classmates, virtually all of whom had been exposed to more language than she had.

At first, she and I concentrated on eliminating the nightmares she had almost every night. Initially, she didn't even understand that they were fantasies. They felt real. When she finally grasped that they were "pretend times," she felt much better. Then I helped her to do a perceptual shift on the monsters in her nightmares. I had her describe them in as much detail as possible, and found out that all she really knew about them was that they were dirty, hairy, and smelly. So we started calling them the Dirty Hairy Smellies. That reduced their dreadfulness by limiting them to just what they were. They were no longer undescribed, no-limitations monsters, who could have had fangs, claws, and other horrible trappings of the nonverbal imagination.

Because they were such powerless monsters, I assured Ally she could kill them during her sleeping pretend time, just by blowing on them really hard. She began to do it with great success, and it endowed her with the first flowering buds of personal power.

Many psychologists and patients, I'm sure, would have tried to find the real-life source of the monsters, but Ally and I didn't have time for that. We had monsters to kill.

There are *always* going to be monsters—for Ally, for me, and for you, too. They are the monsters of loss, death, loneliness, and pain. Monsters are part of life. And it's acceptable to have them in your life—as long as you know how to blow them away.

Ally was exorcising her monsters with her newly discovered cognitive power. But there was also a monster in her waking life, and he, too, needed to be overcome. His name was Ronnie.

To me, Ronnie was just a naughty little kid with his own problems, but to Ally he was an absolute ghoul. He was a long-legged 11-year-old who had lived at the School for the Deaf for about 2 years, and was somewhere between being a leader and a bully. One of his specialties was to gather a group of kids around him and teach them to swear in sign language. It sounds mundane—but a lot of these deaf kids were really sensitive and impressionable. Vulgarity was foreign to them. Sometimes I saw them walking away from Ronnie's playground group looking stunned.

For some reason, Ronnie particularly enjoyed showing the dark side of life to Ally. One day, she asked me what "Go to hell" meant. Trust me, that's not a pleasant concept to introduce to anybody. Even my soft-soap version made Ally's face fall.

Another time, he introduced her to the playground tradition of name-calling ("Farmer Girl! Farmer Girl!"), and shortly after that, he told her the clothes she was wearing were "old-fashioned." She knew what he was saying was true, and it had never bothered her before, but this was another way of looking at it.

The playground monitor taught the kids to say, "Sticks and stones can break my bones, but words can never hurt me." It didn't fly. Words were everything to these kids. They'd left their homes to learn them, and they knew their power.

Ally was sinking. More tantrums than ever. A wary look never left her eyes.

I intervened, and hired Ronnie as my "assistant" during recess. I invented little jobs for him, paid him out of my own pocket, and started showering him with words of praise and encouragement, even when he didn't deserve them. As far as he knew, I considered him the nicest, smartest kid in school. And, by God, over time he started to act like it.

Meanwhile, I shepherded Ally into a relationship with the sweetest little girl in the school, a teacher's daughter who by cruel coincidence had been born deaf (due to post-rubella syndrome, the same as Ally). This little girl, Shari Ann, didn't have a bad word to say about anybody, and she was exactly what Ally needed. I saw them together everywhere, talking and giggling. Once they ran up to me, holding hands, and Ally showed me a new phrase she'd learned. She said, "Shari Ann best friend. Ever and always." She signed it with a flourish, as if it were a prayer made real in the world.

Ally gradually began to become the person that was deep inside her, beneath her layers of protection: a friendly, happy girl, in love with her own life.

Because she had finally begun to make so much progress, I was shocked one day when I came across her sitting on a bench outdoors, looking crestfallen. She didn't notice me as I walked toward her.

With her hands in her lap, she was talking to herself in sign language.

"What is it wrong with me?" she signed. "What is it wrong with me? What is it wrong with me?" She said it again and again, until tears started dropping onto her hands.

Changing Your Language and Changing Your Life

When deaf people talk to themselves in sign language, it activates the same area of the brain, the left interior frontal cortex, that is activated when hearing people talk to themselves. Because this area is adjacent to the brain's primary area of higher thought, and because words make ideas real, engaging in self-talk enables all people, deaf or hearing, to make sense of their thoughts and gain access to their own wisdom.

Since self-talk is so powerful, however, it's important to choose your words carefully. If you use destructive language, you'll muddy your wisdom and create perceptions that can ruin your life.

A good rule to follow in self-talk is to talk to yourself the way you want others to talk to you. Many people would never let other people berate them, and yet they talk to themselves like dogs. They tell themselves, "You're fat!" or "You're gonna screw up!" They think they're challenging themselves to do better, but all they're doing is pushing themselves down the path of fear.

Unhappy people also pervert the power of self-talk by painting unrealistically ugly verbal pictures of their world. They tell themselves, "Nobody understands me," or "My boss is crazy," or "This town is boring."

Sometimes, when people start bashing themselves or the world, I cut them off and ask them to talk about their kids. Their tone changes and their word choice reverses as they begin to rhapsodize about their wonderful children. Then I say, "That's the way you should talk about yourself." Sometimes they get it, and sometimes they don't.

I pay painstaking attention to the language people use; it reveals more than they realize. If it's full of destructive words and phrases, I know they're trapped in the fear response, even if they're trying to project an image of confidence.

You, too, can gain insight by listening carefully to language. The chart on the opposite page gives some examples of constructive language and destructive language. Tune in to language, and you'll learn a lot about people. Even more important, tune in to your own language, especially your self-talk, and you'll learn a lot about yourself.

CONSTRUCTIVE LANGUAGE	DESTRUCTIVE LANGUAGE
One possibility is . . .	You never . . .
It would be good to . . .	There's no way . . .
I love you when . . .	You should . . .
Thank you for . . .	I'm not good at . . .
I appreciate the . . .	What's the point of . . .
I like . . .	The problem with . . .
I understand why . . .	You don't understand . . .
Your best quality . . .	That's stupid . . .
People like you and me . . .	Don't go there . . .
The best part is . . .	It hurts to . . .
Have confidence . . .	He doesn't get it . . .
Please . . .	We'll lose if . . .
We'll succeed if we . . .	I'm better than . . .
It's okay to . . .	Listen to me . . .
My reasoning is . . .	Don't start . . .
I'm best at . . .	Would it kill you to . . .
The good news is . . .	It's depressing when . . .
Let's make the best of . . .	When I was your age . . .
That's a good point . . .	I'm afraid that . . .
How can I help with . . .	This is the worst thing that . . .
I'm sorry . . .	I don't care about . . .
It's my responsibility . . .	You make me . . .

The Power of Language

People who are stuck in fear are often fixated on destructive language. Their conversations are full of "can't," "don't," "shouldn't," and "won't." They also tend to describe their own actions in the passive voice, instead of the active. In addition, they ask questions that beg for negative responses. Sometimes these word choices are subtle, but often they're so grating that you can hardly stand to listen.

However, I've noticed that when people begin to change, their language changes, too. The negatives fall away, the passive descriptions are replaced by active ones, and the "no" questions give way to "yes" questions.

Furthermore, just as changing your life can change your language, changing your language can change your life. It can alter your perceptions and thought processes. Even something as simple as calling an unexpected situation a possibility instead of a problem can change the whole way you look at it. For example, when I started calling Ally's monsters Dirty Hairy Smellies, it didn't change what they were, but it sure changed how Ally felt about them. Similarly, if you start calling your boss challenging instead of demanding, it will change your perspective. Language is so powerful!

Some people, though, take the power of language all the way to la-la land and indulge in the popular nonsense of affirmations. In most cases, affirmations are just verbal gimmicks aimed at refuting what's really going on. They don't reflect reality; they distort it. For example, a common affirmation for a salesman might be, "I'm going to make a lot of money today." Oh, yeah—says who? In real life, you don't know, and if you pretend to, you're just playing mind games and setting yourself up for a fall. Realistically, all you can say is, "I'm going to work hard today." But you don't need an affirmation for that—you just need to do it. Affirmations are usually just a way of whistling past the graveyard.

And if you disagree with me, I really don't care—because I'm good enough, I'm smart enough, and doggone it, people like me.

When I saw Ally crying and signing to herself, I could have spoonfed her an affirmation. I could have urged her to change "What's wrong with me?" into "There's nothing wrong with me!" But that would never have hit home, because she knew something in her life was wrong, and no talk could erase it.

So instead I just asked, "Why are you crying?"

"Shari Ann says mommy and daddy love kids. But my daddy, no. Daddy doesn't love."

It was true. I hadn't seen much of Pa over the past year, but what I had seen had been sickening. He had no appreciation for the tremendous progress she'd made, and he treated her like a stranger.

Some psychologists might have told Ally, "He loves you in his own way." Or, "It doesn't matter." Or, "You don't need him anymore." But I'm not in the baloney business.

"Mommy loves you," I signed.

She began to cry again, but it was a different kind of crying.

I held her. "Mommy loves you."

The Story of Your Life

I told Rita she should leave her husband. Sometimes I do that with people. It shocks the hell out of them. They're accustomed to psychologists who talk to them about their *feelings*, not their lives. I remember about a year ago, a TV star was in my office telling me in 25 million words or less all the things that were wrong with her husband, and how she yearned to be free of him and the pain he caused. At the end of the diatribe I said, "I'm sold. I think you should walk." And she had a cow! How *dare* I destabilize her marriage! She's still with him, still miserable, and still gets mad at me whenever I tell her to do something about it.

Rita had about the same reaction when I mentioned divorce. I saw her frequently, because I translated Ally's sign language whenever she came to the school. She still hadn't learned to sign, and it wasn't just because her husband had ordered her not to. Signing is hard. The kids still laughed at the "accent" I had.

Rita assured me that she just couldn't leave Pa, because she had nowhere to go, no way to make a living, and besides, it wouldn't be fair to Ally to have just one parent. She couldn't get that last reason out with a straight face, though—she laughed at herself even as she said it. Somewhere beneath all of that cornpone submissiveness, she had a lot of heart. I liked her.

"I should'na married so young," she said. "Now I'm just 'bout stuck." She sighed from deep inside. "Story a my life." It was one of her favorite phrases. Victims tend to use it a lot.

"That's one way to tell the story of your life," I said. "Here's another. A woman gets married too young, makes big sacrifices for her daughter, and realizes she's stronger than she thought."

"That's me, too, I guess."

Both stories were true. Rita could spend the rest of her life living out either one. The question was, which one worked?

We all have different ways in which we can tell the story of our lives. Some work, and some don't. I call the ones that work healthy stories, and the ones that don't horror stories.

When you meet someone new and tell him the quick version of the story of your life, do you usually tell him a healthy story or a horror story? Most people want to tell a healthy story, because nobody wants to look bad. But many people just don't know how. They're so accustomed to telling themselves horror stories in their self-talk that they just start blurting out all their fears and feelings of helplessness, although they often cloak them in terms of humor or heroics. They like their job—but it was a real struggle to get it, and it still feels precarious. Their children are doing well—but they're teenagers, and you know how *that* is. They like living here—but it's not the same as home. Then these people wonder why others don't enjoy or admire them more.

Like anyone else, I can tell my own life story as either a healthy story or a horror story—and they're both equally true. Here's the healthy version: I had a good, small-town childhood in the Midwest and now work at a great job in a beautiful place. I spend most of my time with my family, love getting outdoors, and am trying to help change the direction of psychology.

But I could just as realistically put it like this: I grew up in corn country and couldn't wait to get out, but where I live now, it's so hot I can't stand it for about half the year. Early on, I became disillusioned with conventional psychology, and now I'm working harder than I probably should at trying to keep psychology from sinking into irrelevance.

If you'd just met me, which one of these stories would make you want to get to know me? Which one do you think makes me happier, and gives me more energy?

How do you tell the story of *your* life? Take a moment and tell yourself the condensed version right now, in about the same way you usually do when you meet people. Don't gild the lily—be honest.

Now, for fun, do it two more ways: the completely healthy way and the horror story way. Again, be honest, or you won't learn anything about yourself.

Hopefully, the way you usually tell it was closer to your healthy story than your horror story. If not, start using the healthy version. It will change the way you see your life.

It's also smart to tell yourself and others healthy stories about all the little incidents of your daily life. If you're late for work, don't tell yourself that your boss is going to kill you and that you're a loser for sleeping late. Tell yourself you're lucky to have a job where you can be late once in a while, and that you're going to use this experience to be more punctual in the future. The horrific version will just make you defensive, while the healthy one will make you appreciative. People will notice the difference.

It's especially important to tell yourself healthy stories when a crisis strikes. That's when you're going to feel like telling yourself horror stories, but if you stop yourself, you can face the crisis with a clear head and with the energy you need to get past it. I knew a man whose worst crisis was horrific: imprisonment in a Japanese POW camp. To hold off his fear and pain, he did his own form of an Appreciation Audit and listed everything he could think of about the camp that was good, such as the camaraderie and free time for card games. He even started the I Like It Here Club. He never stopped suffering, but he never again saw his suffering in the same way.

Just last week, I had two women in my office who revealed the power of stories. They were both in their mid-twenties, had high incomes and good educations, and even looked fairly similar. They both had problems they considered serious. One had cancer. The other had pimples.

The young woman with cancer had also recently lost her husband in a fatal car wreck. I thought she would want to vent her grief and fear. But the way she told it, she was one lucky young woman! She'd survived the wreck herself, had enough money to get the best treatment, she could afford to take time off from work, the survival rate for her cancer was favorable, and she felt blessed to have known her husband. All she really needed from me was information on using the mind to enhance immunity.

Her language was constructive and her stories were healthy. They weren't delusional. They were true, and that's what gave them power.

The other woman had a moderate case of acne. No scarring or pitting, just some dots of pimples here and there that she concealed with makeup. But to hear her describe it, she was the Phantom of the Opera. Her exact language was, "I'm a hideous monster." The story she'd concocted was that no one would ever love her and that she was doomed to die alone. The longer she talked, the more she talked herself into it. After an hour, she almost had *me* believing it. It was strange, but by the time she left, I was seeing a lot more acne than when she'd arrived.

That's the power of stories.

Rita's Story

My breath caught when I saw Rita standing in my doorway with a suitcase.

"Well, I did it," she said. "I left him."

"Was it hard?"

"He smacked me around, if that's what you mean. Wasn't the first time. But it was the last."

"Are you going to live here in town?"

She nodded. "Shari Ann's mom, Peggy, helped me find a little place. And she got me a job, working here in the office." She swallowed. "I never did office work before. But I keep telling myself, 'If you can get away from that old man, you can do pretty near anything.'"

"Just keep telling yourself that. Because it's true."

"Where's that little girl a mine? I can't wait to tell her."

"I'll call her classroom teacher right now."

Ally arrived looking tentative, uncertain about why she'd been pulled out of class.

"Ally," I signed to her, "your mommy is going to move here. You can live with her while you go to school."

Ally looked wary. "Daddy?" she signed, looking at me, and looking at her mother.

To my astonishment, Rita made the sign for "father," and shook her head, no.

Ally gushed out a deep breath—a breath she seemed to have been holding her whole life—and began to smile a smile that made her whole face radiant.

Rita pointed at herself, crossed her palms over her heart, and pointed at Ally. "I love you."

For the first time, Ally spoke. Her voice was monotone, hard to understand, and beautiful. She said, "Me love," and touched Rita's face.

They grasped hands, at last fully and forever in each other's lives, and at first I thought they were going to cry, but they both started to laugh, and to dance in a circle—a two-person ring-around-the-rosie—laughing and spinning, laughing and spinning, laughing and spinning. Forever together. Best friends. Ever and always.

CHAPTER NINE

The Good Life

I really am quite happy," she said. "I've got good self-esteem." But the dull way she said it betrayed the truth. She knew the words of happiness, but not the music.

Besides, she had cortisol eyes.

Cortisol eyes, puffy and shadowed, come from chronic oversecretion of the big, beefy, hormonal brother of adrenaline. Cortisol is the stuff you start secreting when it's already 5 o'clock, but you're still looking at overtime, a long commute, making dinner, washing the dishes, picking up the house, and collapsing (then it's the stuff that won't let you sleep).

Cortisol erodes immunity, burns the stomach lining, irritates the kidneys, contributes to Alzheimer's, enlarges the adrenal glands—and keeps America running. It's as American as black coffee and big cars.

As cortisol gradually destroys your body, accounting for many of the signs of aging, it also frays your nerves and causes you to swell with a subtle, water-heavy false fat. In the tissue under the eyes, this swelling causes dark, age-revealing circles.

Emily, who was trying so hard to convince me that she was happy, was still in her thirties, but no longer looked it. As a general rule, unhappy people look older than they are. A lot of it is just the way they act, but they also often have certain physical characteristics, such as cortisol eyes, excess weight, and signs of listlessness, enervation, and fatigue. Being unhappy decimates energy, because it's the worst possible stress. When you're happy, effort is easy, and energy spent is energy earned.

For the most part, unhappy people are also more prone to illness than happy people. Chronic long-term stress—which these days is almost synonymous with unhappiness—shuts down the immune system as it revs up the adrenal, fight-flight-freeze reaction.

"Are you winning at life?" I asked Emily. That's sort of a trick question I often ask people, so purposefully vague that it's a veritable verbal inkblot test. If they ask me what I mean, it often indicates that they're not happy. Happy people almost always think they're winning, even when they don't know *what* they're winning.

"I'm not sure what you're asking."

Bad sign. "I basically mean, how are you doing at the three most important elements of your life? Your sense of purpose. Your health. Your relationships. Those are the basics of multidimensional living—you know, a full life. Hardly anybody's happy without a full life."

She pondered it as she inspected her freshly manicured hands, the result of a little Canyon Ranch pampering. "My relationships. Haven't got one. That's why I'm here, to figure out what I'm doing wrong. My sense of purpose—for me, that's my career; it's going well. My health: fine."

"Tell me the nutshell version of the story of your life."

"Okay. I'm doing a job—trying to do a job—that my father thought I could never handle. High school chemistry teacher—and I'm up for a principal's position, as we speak. Dad's jealous, is the real truth—he worked in a vacuum cleaner shop all his life and never thought his little girl would do better than he did. But he ought to be glad about it, because I've been helping my sister take care of him ever since Mom passed away. Plus, I've got a 15-year-old son, and he's testing every limit in the book right now—rebel without a clue. My ex never sees him, so I'm the bad guy, right? He's already talking about girls. I grew up boy crazy myself, and you can see where it got me. But God, I know teachers who'd kill for my position, so I can't complain. It's *time* that's murdering me. How do you raise a teenager, grade papers all night, take care of a dad, find a guy, and get a promotion, all at once? Did I mention stay on a diet? How?" She threw up her hands. Her nails were the color of ripe plums.

She reminded me of someone—somebody who hadn't been as happy as he'd claimed to be, but hadn't been as unhappy as he'd thought. Who was it? I see so many people.

"You just put your finger on one of the biggest problems there is," I said, "building a full life without making yourself crazy."

She seemed pleased, as if she'd given the right answer on a quiz. But I wasn't pleased. I was hearing a lot of things that made me concerned: negative language, a horror story version of her life, a lack of appreciation for what she had, a feeling of having no choices, a preoccupation with her weaknesses, and no real sense of taking responsibility with personal power.

I was also hearing the single most common cry of the American people: My job is killing me! We work to survive—obeying our most primal instinct—but then we find that *the things we do to survive are the things that end up killing us.*

Millions of people kill themselves by putting all their energy into just one dimension of life—usually work—and end up with the disease I call unidimensional living: a one-track life. It's fatal—not always physically, but it's fatal.

"I think maybe you're not as happy as you're letting on," I said.

At just that gentle remark, her eyes went glossy with tears, and she started to say something but choked it back. She took a deep breath, and blurted, "I'm trying as hard as I can, okay? I just don't have *time*, like I told you. Do you have any idea how much time it took to save the money to come here? Did you know I'm missing my son's birthday to be here?"

"Then you really must want to be here."

"I thought I did."

She sat quietly, resenting me, resenting herself, afraid to change, and even more afraid not to. The thing she seemed to need most—multidimensional living—was sitting right in her lap, but she didn't know it. She was an inch away from the good life, and dying every day.

I felt as if I'd known her before. Who was it she reminded me of?

I sat there for a moment, spacing out, and then I knew who it was. It was me.

Purpose

Some time ago, my 9-year-old son sat down next to me at the breakfast table on a Sunday morning, as I was gulping orange juice and getting ready to sprint out the door to run a relationship seminar for families. "Slow down, Dad," Jeremy said, "your families have seen you all week. I haven't seen you since last Sunday."

Ouch! Leave it to a kid to spot hypocrisy. Here I was, telling everybody how to be happy, but not taking my own medicine. Under the surface, it had been gnawing at me, though I'd pushed it down to forge ahead: I was on a mission—to save everybody but me.

That was the end of my obsession with work, and the beginning of my own multidimensional living. Over time, I realized my life was better than I'd thought, if I just took time to live it. I spent more time with my family and worked harder at my health. A quiet contentment began to settle over me.

But it was hard to back away from work, because I was an achievement junkie. I still remember the times early in my career, working at a cardiac care unit, when this great old nurse who'd seen it all would say, "Dr. Baker, we have a patient with a severe anxiety problem—can you see what you can do?" And I'd go talk to the guy for a while, maybe do an Appreciation Audit, and watch his Holter monitor as his blood pressure and heart rate went down. Then the nurse would come by and say, "We've *never* had anyone like *you* before." And I'd feel like Superman! It was like heroin in my veins, a balm against my fear of not being enough.

More accurately, the intoxicating elixir in my veins was a mix of stimulating catecholamine neurotransmitters (including dopamine), energizing hormones (adrenaline and noradrenaline), and stress-induced natural opiates (endorphins and enkephalins). Most of the time, at that early stage of my career, I was able to keep this mix of contentment chemicals under control, because I was experiencing healthy levels of stress. Believe it or not, a little stress—which doctors call eustress—is good for you. Eustress feels challenging and exhilarating, because you feel confident that you can succeed. Eustress induces the secretion of just the right amount of stimulating chemicals—a little adrenaline, a little dopamine, some endorphins, and not much else. But when a challenge begins to feel insurmountable, it mutates into the emotional misery and murderous biochemistry of stress.

Unfortunately, there is often a fine line between challenge and stress. Even when you lead with your strengths—which is one of the best ways to keep challenges manageable—your goals can easily mount faster than you can meet them. If you can't keep up with your own self-imposed pace, your strengths can become your vulnerability.

When this calamity occurs, the usual suspect is time. The mantra of the new millennium is "I don't have time. I don't have time. I don't have time."

Lack of time is now commonly blamed for the increasing incivility in many workplaces. One recent poll found that almost one-fourth of all people are chronically "angry or somewhat angry" at work. In another poll, 42 percent of employees reported verbal abuse by others, 29 percent had screamed at coworkers, 23 percent had cried over job issues, and 10 percent had directly witnessed workplace violence.

Millions of time-obsessed people feel victimized by what I call the Alice Syndrome. In *Alice in Wonderland*, the Queen of Hearts tells Alice, "My dear, here we must run as fast as we can, just to stay in place. And if you wish to go anywhere, you must run twice as fast as that."

I hope you're not expecting me to express pity about how little time there is in the modern world, because the clear fact is, there's as much of it now as there ever was. There are still 24 hours in every day, for every person.

The real scarcity these days is a lack of clear, value-based priorities. We're programmed by fear to want everything—"I'm not enough! I don't have enough!" Thus, we stand perpetually at a crossroads, as does Alice, when she asks the Cheshire Cat, "Which road shall I take?" And the cat says, "That depends on where you want to go." Alice tells him, "I don't know where I want to go." And the cat says, "Well, then, any road will do."

Any road will do! Good advice if you don't know where you're going. Of course, if you actually want to *get* somewhere, any road will *not* do. To get to happiness, or anywhere else, you've got to decide what you really want, and then put your energy where it will do the most good. If you do that, you'll find plenty of time.

As I mentioned to Emily, practically everybody has only three basic interests in life: their sense of purpose (which is usually their work), their health, and their relationships (with other people and with God). After these concerns, the rest is trivial.

Many people, unfortunately, get hooked on happiness trap trivialities—everything from status seeking to wanton wanting to couch spudding—and they lose touch with their true selves and what they truly want. When this happens, they forfeit their chance for happiness.

Many others have the good sense to stick closely to the big three elements, but still can't manage to accommodate all three in their lives.

When I first started out as a counselor, I followed the party line of clinical psychology and told my clients they should find balance among these three basic elements. What a fiasco! I had people telling me, "Hey, I started spending more time with my family and less at work, and guess what? I got fired!" Or, "I balanced my life, like you said, and now I'm bored as hell."

Back to the drawing board. The more I thought about it, the more I saw how different people are. Some of them live for love, some live for work, and some live for that high, whole feeling of great health. But virtually nobody is fulfilled when they live a unidimensional life, existing only for work, only for others, or only to get buff at the gym. People just aren't built for that. We're too complex.

The key to fulfillment is to integrate all three elements into every day, and then let your passions take you where they may. If your passion is for other people, immerse yourself in that—but don't drown in it. Save some of yourself for your work and some for your health. That's the only way to be a complete human being. I'm sure you know people who've gotten carried away with just one aspect of their lives and seemed to be happy. But those people almost always have a reservoir of regret. They say, "I'm married to my job, but I wish I'd had kids." Or, "I love my family, but I always wonder what would have happened if I'd kept working."

In these declarations of regret, people often indulge in the blame game and cite the tyranny of time, but time is never the villain. You have, quite literally, all the time in the world. You have exactly as much time as the richest person in the world, the most powerful person, and the wisest person: 24 hours each day. Time is not a tyrant. Time is the great equalizer.

The real culprit is making decisions that are driven by fear: choosing too much, choosing a happiness trap as a priority, or not choosing at all. These are the actions that squander time and render it scarce.

But time needn't be scarce. When you make the right choices—inspired by love instead of fear—you end up doing what you love, and time becomes abundant. Studies of the subjective sense of time show that when people are engaged in things they love, time flows at the pace they dictate: fast and furious, or slow and luxurious.

When you hate what you're doing, though, time crawls, and then suddenly evaporates, as another day slides into oblivion. This happens when people follow money instead of their passions and sense of purpose. They think they're being practical—even heroic—but they're just suckers falling for the tricks of the money trap.

Some people let themselves get stuck in jobs just because the jobs are easy or safe. But an easy job without satisfaction is the hardest job of all, and the biggest risk is taking *no* risks.

Others think they can escape stress by not working at all. But that means living a life without purpose, and that's like trying to live on cotton candy. Boredom is one of the worst possible stressors.

Your sense of purpose doesn't need to be monumental. You don't need to cure cancer. In the last years of my grandfather's life, he grew roses, and he did it with so much passion and precision that it totally fulfilled him.

Entertainment legend George Burns, whose own sense of purpose helped him to live to 100, offered advice as wise as any philosopher's: "Every day, do something you love."

Here are some questions that might help you clarify your sense of purpose. Don't just read them. Answer them. Then ask yourself: Am I living a life I love?

◆ What brings vitality to your life?
◆ What do you want to be known as?
◆ What's your proudest achievement?
◆ What does your life stand for?

- What would you sacrifice your life for?
- In what situation do you feel most alive?
- What would you want on your tombstone?

Hearing the Voice of the Heart

"I don't know how to feel," Emily said, breathless with nerves. "Too much is happening!"

"What's going on?"

"One good thing, one bad. That principal opening—it's mine, if I want it. That's the good thing. But I just got an abnormal Pap result from your lab—and my mom died from cervical cancer. Young—not much older than me. So I should focus on the good thing, right?"

"Not necessarily. They're both real."

"Thanks a bunch."

"The most important thing about the Pap smear is to keep it from becoming something it's not. When scary things like that happen, you've got to look at them through your intellect and spirit, not your automatic fear response. If you look through the eyes of fear, it can carry you away. But if you don't, you might get something good out of this."

"Such as?"

"Such as facing down your fear of what killed your mom. It's probably been on your mind ever since she died."

"It has."

"This is your chance to wrestle with it. I know you'd rather not have to, but it's there, and if you do it well, you could come out of this with less fear than you've had for quite a while."

"That'd be good. It *is* just an abnormality, though. The doctor said it's common." She looked better. It's amazing how well the intellect and spirit can overpower fear.

"We have great doctors here," I said. In fact, Canyon Ranch has some of the most prominent M.D.'s in the country, fully supported by a cadre of chiropractors, herbalists, psychologists, physiologists, exercise therapists, massage therapists, nurses, technicians, rehabilitation specialists—you name it: 700 staff members for 250 guests. As the director of the Life Enhancement Program, I help see that Ranch guests get the broad spectrum of care that people need to not just ward off illness, but achieve the vibrant thrill of great health. We approach physical health at the Ranch the same way we do mental health: We don't settle for climbing from a negative ten to zero. We zoom past zero without even stopping and shoot for a plus ten. Even then, the sky's the limit. Our guests, by nature, are ambitious people, looking for the best life can offer.

"Let's talk about that principal's job," Emily said. That quickly, she'd set aside her cancer fear. If she'd let herself feed into it—in the guise of resolving it—it would have led her down a road that has no end.

"What are the pros and cons of the job?" I asked.

"The pro is more money. The con is that I prefer teaching."

"Prefer it a lot more?"

"Hands down. I'm a very good teacher."

"How much do you need the money?"

"It'd be nice. But we're getting by."

"Would your dad be proud of you?"

"That's not a factor. Like you said the other day, I can't control how he feels."

People can change so quickly! Only 6 days into a 2-week stay, Emily was already telling healthier stories and gaining personal power. And if she chose to let it, this cancer scare could heighten her appreciation and hone her sense of priorities. Sometimes people need a crisis to blast them out of their false, exterior security and into the true security of the inner self.

"My opinion?" I said. "I think you should teach. I think that's what your heart is telling you to do."

She looked surprised. It shocks people when a psychologist walks out on a limb and offers an actual opinion.

She began to smile. It came from the inside.

There was a knock on the door. It was my secretary, Dellina. "I have some test results."

"My mammogram," Emily said. "I told them to send the results here."

She was still smiling as she opened the envelope. Scanned the letter. Her face drained to the color of skim milk.

"Oh, my God. They want a biopsy."

Health

It took me about a second and a half to jump to the conclusion that the problems on Emily's two tests were related—and therefore serious—but by the time I arrived at that fear, Emily was already there, waiting.

If there was a connection, she told me in a hollow voice, it could indicate metastases, which probably meant: terminal. Before she even finished her sentence, she had herself dead and buried.

I pulled myself away from the automatic fear reaction. That path is always there, but you don't always have to take it.

As I stepped back and looked at the situation more rationally, I realized that the two problems were probably coincidental. But it was harder, of course, to pull Emily off the path of fear—not just because she had so much more to lose, but also because she had less practice at managing fear. Over the years, even when the lives of those I've loved have been on the line, I've learned how to stay strong by using the forces of the mind and spirit: appreciation, choice, responsibility, strengths, healthy stories, and multidimensional living.

These forces—even more than an easy life—are the best defenses against fear. The good life comes and goes, but the forces of the spirit endure forever.

I wanted to say something encouraging. But the best I could do was, "You can be happy, even with cancer."

"You sound like a Hallmark card. Written by Kafka."

I couldn't help but laugh, and that got her to laugh, too. Her face brightened, as the brief burst of humor helped disengage her fear reaction.

"I know it sounds weird," I said, "but I meet a lot of really sick people who are more full of life than healthy people. You wouldn't believe the diversity of health I see every Monday morning, when we welcome the new guests. I see people in wheelchairs and people who are mountain climbers, and sometimes it's hard to tell who feels healthier."

In fact, though I didn't mention it to Emily, I've met people dying of cancer who radiated vitality. And I've known people with no illness at all who dragged around as if every step hurt, looking at the world through eyes as dull as those of a dead fish.

The key to feeling healthy is simple: Appreciate the health you have, and show your appreciation by doing as much with it as you can.

Sometimes when I tell this to people, they look relieved, as if they're thinking, "Good! I was afraid you'd tell me to lose weight or stop smoking." But they're ignoring the part about *doing* what you can. Nobody gets out of my office without doing something.

It is, of course, possible to mentally rise above ill health—it's even heroic. But that's still just the second-best way to feel healthy. The best way is to actually *be* healthy.

There's no secret about what health requires. Basically, it means doing what your mom always told you: Eat your vegetables, watch the sweets, get fresh air and exercise, stay away from cigarettes, don't stay up too late, and don't sweat the small stuff. These days, this general prescription can also include some esoteric measures—everything from acupuncture to herbal medicine—but the basics are the same as ever. Always will be.

If you put in the effort, you can achieve my favorite definition of health, coined by Jesse Williams, M.D., in the 1920s: "Health is the optimal condition of being that allows for the ultimate engagement with life." Of course, this definition means that health is more than simply the absence of disease. That sounds strange to some people. But does the absence of poverty mean wealth? Does the absence of panic mean peace of mind?

This is an ambitious definition, but it's within reach of everyone. Each of us can make the most of the health we have. Some of the guests at the Ranch can hike up the surrounding Santa Catalina Mountains, while others can only walk in the therapy pool, but practically everybody gets out there and does what he can.

One major reason we emphasize physical health so much in the Life Enhancement Program is because it's very important for mood. As I've mentioned, happiness is much more than a good mood, but it's very hard to feel your happiness under the cloud of a dark mood. I've known hundreds of people who had happy lives but didn't even know it, because they'd trashed their mood chemistry with a poor diet, inactivity, too much booze, or failure to take a mild antidepressant.

In fact, it appeared as if mood was one of Emily's problems. She seemed to have a mild anxiety disorder, and it magnified all her real-world problems. However, when she started exercising, taking some supplements, and cutting out her reliance on sweets, her mood improved appreciably. She still had the same problems, but she saw them from a more buoyant point of view.

Here's a quick rundown of the mood modalities that I recommend to guests at the Ranch.

Food and Mood

Blood glucose instability is a huge problem that affects the moods of millions of people. The brain accounts for only about 2 percent of body weight, but requires 25 percent of all blood pumped by the heart (up to 50 percent in kids). Therefore, low blood sugar hits the brain hard, causing depression, anxiety, and lassitude. If you often become uncomfortably hungry, you've got a serious problem and should solve it. Eat high-protein, nutrient-dense meals, and snack enough to keep your blood sugar up, but not with insulin-stimulating sweets or starches. Remember that hunger kills brain cells, just like getting drunk. Be careful of caffeine, which causes blood sugar swings, and never crash diet.

Food sensitivities are common reactions that are not classic food allergies, so most conventional allergists underestimate the damage they do. They play a major role in mood disruption, much more frequently than most people realize. They cause chemical reactions in the body that destabilize blood sugar and wreak havoc upon hormonal and neuro-transmitter balance. This can trigger depression, anxiety, impaired concentration, insomnia, and hyperactivity.

The most common sensitivities, unfortunately, are to the foods people most often overconsume: wheat, milk, eggs, corn, soy, and peanuts. The average American gets about 75 percent of her calories from just 10 favorite foodstuffs, and this narrow range of eating disrupts the digestive process and causes abnormal reactions. If a particular food doesn't agree with you and commonly causes heartburn, gas, bloating, water weight gain, a craving for more, or a burst of nervous energy, you're probably reactive to it. There are several good books on the subject, and there are many labs that test for sensitivities. Ask a chiropractor, naturopath, or doctor of integrative medicine about them. Don't expect much help from a conventional allergist.

Exercise and Mood

Dozens of studies indicate that exercise is often as effective for depression as medication, partly because it increases production of stimulating hormones, such as norepinephrine, and also because it increases oxygen flow to the brain. Exercise can, in addition, help relieve and prevent anxiety, creating a so-called tranquilizer effect that persists for about 4 hours after exercising. Exercise also decreases the biological stress response, which dampens the automatic fear reaction. It is also uniquely effective at causing secretion of Nerve Growth Factor, one of the limited number of substances that cause brain cells to grow. Another benefit of exercise is that it increases endorphin output by about 500 percent and decreases the incidence of major and minor illnesses. For mood, the ideal amount is 30 to 45 minutes of cardiovascular exercise daily. Studies show that exercising less than 30 minutes or more than 1 hour decreases mood benefits.

Nutritional Supplements and Mood

The people who claim you can get all the nutrients you need from your diet alone must eat a lot of rutabagas, chicory, and sardines. In the real world, this just doesn't happen. To protect your mood chemistry, you particularly need the unique micronutrients that your body uses to manufacture neurotransmitters. For production of acetylcholine (the primary neurotransmitter of thought), take daily dosages of lecithin (5,000–10,000 mg), vitamin C (1,000–2,000 mg), and B_5 (100 mg); for dopamine (an important feel-good neurotransmitter), take tyrosine (500 mg), phenylalanine (500 mg), and moderate amounts of folic acid, magnesium, vitamin C, and B_{12}; for serotonin (the primary contentment neurotransmitter), take 5-HTP (a derivative of tryptophan). All of these nutrients may be purchased at health food stores.

The most important individual mood nutrients include the B-complex vitamins—especially B_{12} (for energy), niacin (for anxiety), and B_6 and folic acid (for depression)—along with vitamins C and E (to restore neurotransmitter receptors), magnesium and calcium (for calmness), 5-HTP (for insomnia, and to increase serotonin), and chromium (for blood sugar stabilization).

The simplest way to get many of these nutrients is to buy a mood-enhancing formulation at a health food store. Individual supplements, however, usually provide higher amounts of nutrients.

It's best to consult a physician who does nutritional therapy, such as a naturopath, some chiropractors, or some M.D.'s. Do not rely mostly on a sales clerk in a store.

Medication and Mood

Pharmaceutical medication for minor to moderate mood problems, once unheard of, has lately become so popular that it is now rather overrated. In particular, the serotonin-enhancing drugs, such as Prozac and Paxil, have helped millions of people, but are too often seen as panaceas. However, when antidepressants are combined with an aggressive program of counseling and lifestyle change, they can often work wonders.

Also beneficial are certain herbal medications. St. John's wort, in one meta-analysis of 23 studies cited in the *British Medical Journal*, was significantly more effective than tricyclic antidepressants for depression. Also, ginkgo biloba is generally believed to increase cerebral circulation, and ginseng has been shown to be moderately effective against depression and fatigue.

Many people also find relief from mood problems with homeopathic remedies, which are available at health food stores. The labels on these products clearly indicate the conditions that the products can help correct. Remember that not all natural products are benign, and that many health food store clerks are poorly informed. *Consult a competent health care professional.*

Striving for health is important, but it can still be overdone. If you're exercising so much that you're often tired from it, are eating a sparse and unenjoyable diet, or are restricting yourself from all possible vices, stop feeling proud of yourself. Perfectionism in health, like all other forms of perfectionism, is a form of fear. Face it: You are going to die. Make sure you live, first.

All Your Life

Emily, scared to death, was coming to life. She was still waiting for her biopsy result, and the crisis was bringing her ever closer to her true self. With a deadly threat hanging over her head, she couldn't afford to indulge in fear. She knew that if she got started, there'd be no end to it. So she was marshalling her spirit and intellect, and it showed in her language, and even in the way she looked. Her eyes were brighter and she'd lost weight, thanks to the Ranch's superb food. Much of it was water weight, which may have come from avoiding reactive foods, or from having less bloat-inducing cortisol in her system.

I complimented her on it. She said, "And just think of the weight loss possibilities of chemo!" She laughed, and I joined her. Dark humor is good against fear.

Emily said she was hoping that if the weight loss continued, it would help her find a guy.

"It will," I said, "but mostly because of how you'll feel about yourself." I've talked to hundreds of women about weight, and the wisest thing I've ever heard is that for attracting guys, it's more important to feel thin than to look thin: Make peace with your body.

"God, I miss having a relationship," she said.

"But you do have a relationship."

"I do?"

"With your son."

"My son," she said flatly. What did that mean?

It meant, she told me, that they weren't close at all anymore. In his life, she ranked about eighth, after basketball, his buddies, Nintendo, some girl in biology class, his motorbike, his Dell, and his newfound sexuality—not in that order.

"He used to tell me all his problems. Now he just gets pissed off. I think anger is just sadness with a penis."

I said it was a stage, and she contradicted me, bitterly. He'd changed, she said. He was cold. Resentful. He didn't need her.

"You like to face facts, right?" she said. "Let's face this one: He doesn't love me anymore. That happens—it happens all the time—and no shrink can tell me it doesn't."

I didn't say anything.

"Why *should* he love me?" The words rushed out of her. "I don't love him anymore, either."

The moment she said it, she looked shocked, as if she'd just slapped herself in the face. Then her expression pinched into fear, as if she were waiting for God's lightning to strike.

"It's true," she said, her voice cold as snow.

"Tell me about a time when you did love him."

She was quiet for at least a minute. Then she said, "I remember the day he was born. That evening. Everything had settled down and nobody was around. Says a lot about my ex, huh? Anyway, I picked up the baby, and he was awake, with these bright little blue eyes, and I'm waiting to feel this big rush of love for him, because I thought that's the way the world goes 'round: You love your kids, and then you're motivated to take care of them, and life goes on. But nothing's happening! No rush of love, no nothing. I'm thinking, What am I—some kind of postpartum freak? Then I get to thinking about my own mom, like, 'How'd you do it, Mom?' 'Cause I've got this mom—I had this mom—who took care of me every day of my life, one way or another. Even when I was an adult, she was still the mom, and I was still her little girl. Even though she's dead, she's still taking care of me, with money she saved, and with letters she left for me to open on each of my next 20 birthdays." She swallowed. "So anyway, I looked down at my baby, and I said to him, 'I promise to take care of you all your life, just like my mom did me.' Then, whoosh! Like a flash flood! This huge wave of love! Washing over me! I've never felt anything like it. Never!"

The wonder of it was still on her face. "I was so surprised. Because I'd been certain that you love somebody first, *then* you take care of them. I was sure of it."

Her face had softened again, and had somehow become more real, as if she'd peeled off yet another mask.

"What did your son say when you told him about the biopsy?"

"Oh, I'd never tell him about something like that. Unless there was a need. Never."

"Why not?"

She looked at me as if I were the world's dumbest man.

"You told me a lie," I said.

"What lie?"

"You told me you didn't love your son."

She started to speak. Couldn't. Tried again.

"Take your time," I said. "We have all the time in the world."

She smiled a mother's smile.

There is a time in the lives of some people—a specific, memorable time—when they turn the corner. When they leave a life dominated by fear and enter a life led by love.

This was Emily's time.

Relationships

Talking about relationships is just another way of talking about love—either love lost or love fulfilled. We can't be human alone.

When I was working in one of the trenches of life and death—a cardiac care unit, where death was common—I found that what people wanted to talk about most was their relationships. Even people who'd built their lives around work spoke movingly of those who had shared their missions.

And yet now, when I talk each day to people whose lives lie largely ahead, I hear incessant horror stories about relationships—ones that are twisted, squandered, on hold, or dead. Sometimes I feel like grabbing people and shaking them awake: *Forget* your deadlines, forget your workout—take your wife to lunch—take your kids to a ball game! Live a little!

But people too often do the opposite. They hit some snags in their relationships, and instead of smoothing them out, they start hiding behind their work, a socially acceptable form of flight. They become infatuated with their achievements and with the money and praise that go with them, and start manufacturing the need to spend ever more hours at the office. Even when they're home, they yawn through their family life as though it were just a long coffee break. Often as not, they expect their families not only to forgive their indifference, but to be grateful for what it produces. Then they bitch about being loved for their money. This is the failure of success.

As a general rule, unidimensional people like this never really learned how to take love beyond its infatuation stage. When they first met their spouses, or first held their newborn children, they got drunk on the biochemical bonding agents of infatuation, such as the hormones oxytocin and phenylethylamine. Then, as the biochemical high wore off, they fell out of love and into reality. They began to see that the objects of their affection were only human. If they were excessively hardwired for hard times, they never got over the shock, and never made the transition to true love. True love comes only through appreciation.

A long time ago, I remember talking to one guest—a successful realtor but an otherwise ordinary guy—who was going on and on about how he really loved his new girlfriend, but she had this little fault and that little fault. She was beautiful, but not quite beautiful enough. She loved sports, but not the way he did. Real deal breakers. Ultimately, he concluded, "She's not the one."

"You're a perfectionist, aren't you?" I asked him.

"Guess I am," he replied, with thinly concealed pride.

"Here's your homework. Tonight, when you go home—look in a mirror."

He didn't get it. He thought I was saying he should try to become even more perfect—*then* he'd attract Miss Right and live happily ever after.

Never happened, of course. People like him are their own unhappy endings.

Other people sabotage relationships by expressing their fear in a different way. Instead of holding out for someone perfect, to make *them* perfect, they assume they'll never have enough or be enough to attract anybody. So they don't even try, and guess what happens? They turn out to be right.

Even that kind of disaster isn't as bad, though, as the punishment people beg for when their fear tells them they're not good enough to marry someone who loves them—so they marry someone who doesn't. Often, in lieu of love, they settle for looks or money—and then wonder why later on they see nothing but flaws. Sometimes people don't even look for compensating qualities, but just go through the motions of attachment, presuming that even a hollow marriage is better than none. It's not. It's just a protective barrier that prevents even the possibility of real love.

The most important relationship of a person's life, though, needn't be a romantic relationship. For example, toward the end of her stay at the Ranch, Emily realized that her relationship with her son might always be the primary relationship of her life, and this realization made her feel great. She felt far less desperate about finding a romantic relationship, in order to fill up a self-proclaimed void. When she found this wisdom in herself, she not only turned down the principal's position, but even cut her schedule to a 30-hour week, to have more time with her son (and when she called her supposedly cold son to tell him, he was thrilled). Even nonromantic relationships offer us the chance to get outside ourselves, and that is the ultimate blessing of any relationship. Getting outside oneself is one of the best ways to be happy. Self-absorption is a prison. It's solitary confinement.

One relationship that always gets us outside ourselves is our relationship with God. God, of course, means very different things to different people. Many people believe in a very literal, intercessionary father figure who watches over them at all times. Many others believe in a creative spirit that is far less personally involved in their own lives. Still others believe that the nature of God is mysterious—even unknowable—existing as an inscrutable positive force—perhaps love. This view was stated eloquently by Carl Jung: "Man can try to name love, showering upon it all the names at his command, and he will still involve himself in endless self-deceptions. If he possesses a grain of wisdom, he will lay down his arms and name the unknown by the more unknown: by the name of God."

Whatever one believes, it's been clearly established that a belief system that adds spiritual meaning to life helps people thrive. Consider the following points. As you note, they apply to members of organized religions; but in my opinion, they probably also apply to most spiritually-inclined people, even if these people are not affiliated with a particular religion.

◆ Numerous studies indicate that people with positive religious beliefs are happier than those who discount religion.
◆ A study of immunity showed that religious people, compared to nonreligious people, had only half as much of a protein that indicates immune weakness (interleukin-6).
◆ Religious people, according to one study, were 40 percent less likely to have high blood pressure than nonreligious people.
◆ In a study of coronary heart disease, religious men had 20 percent less incidence than nonreligious men.

There is one other relationship in people's lives that is of paramount importance: their relationship with themselves. But many people don't even know it exists.

I often ask new guests at the Ranch to describe their relationships with their spouses, siblings, and parents, and I almost always get quick, straightforward answers. Then I say, "Tell me about your relationship with yourself." Often as not, they go blank. Then they stammer out some generalization.

Many people think there's no such thing as a relationship with oneself: There's only one me, so how can *I* have a relationship with *me*? Actually, there's more than one you. There's the parent you, the child you, the professional you, the spiritual you, etc. There's also the core you, the part of you that is most central and most indestructible. The core you is always passing judgments and giving advice to the other aspects of your selfhood. It happens dozens of times a day.

These judgments and this guidance must be rooted in the qualities that create happiness: appreciation, personal power, a recognition of strengths, and a sense of choice. The judgments and advice must be conveyed with constructive language and framed within healthy stories. This is imperative. This is the foundation of a healthy relationship with oneself. It's one of the first steps on the road to happiness.

Emily, in just the 2 weeks since I'd first met her, had developed a new relationship with herself. She was no longer her own worst enemy nor her most fervent apologist. Over this short time, she had learned to love herself—not by delving into herself and her past, but by going outside herself, welcoming the world in, and finding the only reality that ever really exists: the reality of the moment, free from fear.

I'll always remember one day with her most clearly. It was the day she got her biopsy result. She'd asked the lab to send it to me, so we could talk about it, if it was bad news.

Emily

"I met a guy! I met a guy!"

"Tell me everything."

"First things first. Look at this!"

Emily pulled a greeting card out of her purse, handling it as if it were treasure.

"Read it." She was beaming. "I just got it. Not 10 minutes ago. Today's my son's birthday."

Printed on the cover was "From Mother to Son on Sweet 16." But it had been altered by a red pen to read "From Son to Mother on Sweet 16."

Inside, in the same red pen, it said, "I don't know why kids get presents from their moms on their birthdays. They're the ones who should be giving the presents." It was signed, "Love you always, Bryan."

"God, I'm so happy," she said.

I held the card in my hands and couldn't help but think of my own little Ryan, my son, gone all these years, who would have been a young man himself now. What would he be like? Like this sweet son of Emily's?

"I had a son named Ryan," I said. I wanted to say more, but this was her time, not mine.

"Tell me about him," Emily said. "We have time."

I told her a few things, at least the parts that made me appreciate his life, and she listened with care and feeling. I could see why she was a fine teacher.

"Oh, my God!" she said. "The biopsy! I forgot about the biopsy."

"Me too."

I pointed at the envelope from the lab on my desk, lying next to the card, and she reached out. But she didn't take it.

She took the card instead, and, smiling, opened it again.

Maybe for good luck.

Epilogue

Going Sane

It was cancer, of course. Damn! Life never lets up, does it? You get to thinking, Wow, I'm finally old enough to feel secure—and life comes along and says, "Yeah, and that means you're old enough to get cancer, too." Or you finally get some money in the bank, and life says, "Sorry—recession!—since you've got money, you've got money to lose."

Fear, fear, endless fear. We've all been there.

Emily, close to panic, her eyes frantic, scanned the biopsy report and said, "What does in-situ carcinoma mean?"

"It means that it hasn't spread. That's *good* news."

She gave me a withering look.

"Do you want me to have your doctor come over?" I asked. "We could talk about your options."

"You mean, what size casket? A large. Unless chemo helps."

It wasn't funny, but I made myself laugh anyway, and even my strangled little laugh seemed to tug her away from pure fear.

Nonetheless, she'd been stopped dead in her tracks. Not moments before, she'd been so uplifted by her son's birthday card that she'd forgotten about her biopsy report. But now she had cancer. Forget the card. Forget the new guy she'd met. She had cancer.

When people are blasted open by hurt, it's easy to see inside them, and looking at Emily, I saw her begin to sink into herself. Her shoulders sagged, her eyes went inward, her hands became busy and white with fear, and her breaths came in short little huffs.

Her face was the color of death. I was losing her.

She was losing herself.

The strong self she'd found over the past 2 weeks seemed suddenly mythical—a movie character, a charade, just a new mask to wear over her old masks of fear and regret.

But I knew that her strengths were every bit as real as her fear. Just harder to find.

I put my hand over her clenched fist. It felt like a snowball. "Emily, a minute ago, you chose love over fear. You've got to keep doing that."

"I've gotten better advice from a *fortune cookie!*"

Caught off guard, this time my laugh was real, and she had the courage to share it. What a heart she had!

"I'm just saying you're in too deep to give in to fear. Do that now, and it may never end."

She closed her eyes. What was behind them, I'll never know.

In every life, there are defining moments—moments that set the course of fate. When they're happening, you're not always aware that they will change you forever. At the time, these moments usually just seem like one more mountain to climb in an endless series of peaks.

And that's all these moments are—if you back off.

If you do back off, you sometimes sit in the shadow of that mountain and wonder, What if? What if I'd asked that woman to marry me? What if I'd finished that project? Made that investment? But then you let the thought pass by: It wasn't meant to be. It wasn't my destiny.

But as I've said, I don't believe in destiny. I believe you decide your own fate every day, by what you do and what you don't.

If you're strong, one fine day you simply say, "I'm going to climb that mountain." And when you do, you see it wasn't just another peak. It was the summit.

And from that summit you can see a multitude of paths leading to the fertile valley of a new life below, cradling a river rich with choice, and you stand not in triumph but in awe: Is this what all that struggle was for? This simple confluence of rock, water, and earth? This uncomplicated ease? This peace?

As you amble down to the life that awaits.

"Lean on your love, Emily. It's the only thing that can get you through this."

"I can't." Her eyes were still tight. "I can't."

"I *know* you, Emily."

All the breath came out of her. She picked up the card again and pressed it against her heart. She took my phone and dialed.

"I got your card," she said. "Of course I did. It was wonderful. I have another present for you. I'm flying you down here for a week. It's so beautiful! You're welcome. I love you, too. I'll call later." She put the phone down gently.

Her face, again, was the color of life.

"I need him now," she said.

"I know you do."

She pushed her palms against her eyes.

After a long time, she looked up. "I think I'm going crazy," she said.

"I could be wrong, but I think you just went sane."

She laughed—she got it—and I knew she really had gone sane, and that live or die, she was back. She was her true self, strong and loving, and not even cancer could kill that.

I've seen people go crazy. Sometimes it happens in outpatient care programs in which they've landed because they're teetering on the brink, caught somewhere between borderline personality disorder and frank psychosis. Occasionally, particularly if it's a young person, or if it's an older person suffering from senile dementia, there is a powerful bio-chemical component to the process. Other times, there is no discrete salient factor in the disintegration of their lives. They just begin to lose that cohesive force, that power of personality, that makes them a unique, individualized being. It's as if they were a shock of cornstalks held to-gether by twine, with the twine slowly unraveling until—pop!—it lets go. And then the cornstalks fall and scatter, and they stay that way, in disarray, no matter how hard anyone tries to gather them back together. Suddenly the person is no longer a person at all, but a case, a diagnosis, another singular soul lost to the darkness.

When you see something like that start to happen, you want to say, "I can help! I can help!" And you *can* help, if you care enough, because the things that hold people together—their twine, so to speak—are things we all have inside, things we can share. They are things like optimism, courage, proactivity, spirituality, humor, altruism, and love.

Love most of all. Love is the saving grace.

If you want to give of these qualities to someone who is teetering on the brink, you can help them pull back from the abyss—help them realize, Hey! This isn't so bad. I can handle this. I've seen worse.

I'm sure you've done this yourself—probably just not with someone who has a diagnosable disorder. Doesn't matter. These qualities don't just help disturbed people from going crazy. They also help healthy people to stay sane, and to *go* sane when troubles seem unsolvable.

Even more important, they help people to be happy. And ultimately, what's the difference between happiness and sanity? Not much. I've never seen a happy person who was crazy (except in movies), and I've never seen a crazy person who was happy.

And yet, so many of us persist in swallowing the old cynical psychology myth that sanity is serious business, while happiness is . . . nothing much . . . pure fluff—just the giggling of little girls.

But think about the people you've met in this book. Were their efforts trivial? Their quests trifling? Think about the man I called Job, who lost everything he loved, but somehow kept his love. Think about Kate, who seemed to be doomed to a purgatory without possibilities, but learned to build bike brakes and fought her way to a real life. Think about the firefighters of September 11, who ran in when everyone else was running out. Think of Christopher Conner, who finally glimpsed his life at the moment of a child's death. And the rock star, who found reality in a world of pretense. My father, whose spirit defies death. Little Ally and her mom, Rita, who learned each other's languages. And Emily, of course Emily.

These are great men and women.

They showed me what happy people know.

And they all found happiness in more or less the same simple way: They chose love over fear. In the dance of the spirit and the reptile, they found a way to let their spirits lead. They tapped the powers of choice, of language and stories, of personal power, of their own signature strengths, and of multidimensional living.

They took the *events* of their lives—often painful, sometimes unbearable—and transformed them into meaningful *experiences*.

Often, they had no idea where their next step would lead. They stared into the chasm of the unknown. It was my honor to stand with them on those days when they peered into the abyss. Shattered people, pioneers of the spirit, they took the leap into the void, into the nothingness, and came out whole. My happiness now is that I was with them then. I helped them find their pilgrim's soul.

To make their steps easier to follow, I've compiled an Action Plan (see page 256). It came from the lives of others, but now it's yours.

This Is Happiness

It was a spring morning, too beautiful to describe. A morning of new life. Not long ago.

(continued on page 258)

THE ACTION PLAN

From Event to Experience: Happiness or Unhappiness?

Event

Higher Brain Response

Emotionally Enhancing Reactions
- Intellect-driven responses
- Spirit-driven responses

Practicing Appreciation (Happiness Tool #1)
- Focusing on love
- Personal Appreciative Inquiry technique
- Freeze Frame technique
- Appreciation Audit technique
- Practicing forgiveness
- Making perceptual shifts
- Practicing altruism

Making Choices (Happiness Tool #2)
- Living proactively
- Using the life-changing quarter-second
- Using the 60-Minute Principle
- Unlearning learned helplessness
- Practicing power over perception
- Exercising free will

Building Personal Power (Happiness Tool #3)
- Taking responsibility
- Rejecting Victimization, Entitlement, Rescue, and Blame (VERB)
- Taking action
- Managing your own emotions
- Practicing optimism

Leading with Your Strengths (Happiness Tool #4)
- Recognizing your weaknesses and accepting them
- Mobilizing your talents
- Accessing your own wisdom
- Constructive Questioning technique
- Best Personal Practices technique

Reptilian Brain Response

Fear-Based Reactions
- Fighting
- Freezing
- Fleeing

Trying to Buy Happiness (Happiness Trap #1)
- Believing money brings freedom
- Seeking happiness through security
- Seeking happiness through status
- Seeking happiness through power
- Seeking happiness through possessions

Trying to Find Happiness through Pleasure (Happiness Trap #2)
- Trudging the hedonic treadmill
- Becoming weak from indulgence
- Trying to kill fear with pleasure
- Inflating expectations

Trying to Resolve the Past (Happiness Trap #3)
- Trying to drain the subconscious of fear
- Overestimating the power of catharsis
- Fighting fear with fear
- Getting stuck in childhood
- Fixating on the VERBs: victimization, entitlement, rescue, and blame

Trying to Overcome Weaknesses (Happiness Trap #4)
- Reinforcing weakness by opposing it
- Doing the Dirty Ds (demanding, devaluing, demeaning, discarding, desperately doubling)
- Ignoring your strengths
- Falling for perfectionism

Employing Constructive Language (Happiness Tool #5)
- Reprogramming the brain linguistically
- Articulating lessons learned
- Voicing appreciation
- Expressing choice

Living Multidimensionally (Happiness Tool #6)
- Integrating life's three basic elements: purpose, health, and relationships
- Using a full-spectrum approach: nutritional therapy, exercise, supplements, and natural and pharmaceutical medications

Healthy Stories
- Are positive about self and others
- Are filled with appreciation
- Are about lessons that were learned
- Are told with constructive language
- Are inspiring to self and others
- Are optimistic

The Emotionally Enhanced Life
Is characterized by:
- Love
- Health
- Optimism
- Spirituality
- Courage
- Altruism
- A sense of freedom
- Perspective
- Proactivity
- A good sense of humor
- Security
- Purpose

Trying to Force Happiness (Happiness Trap #5)
- Seeing happiness as an end in itself, rather than a byproduct
- Trying to find happiness through force of will
- Using affirmations and other feel-good gimmicks
- Trying to be happy without changing

Horror Stories
- Are negative about self and others
- Are about problems that were suffered
- Are pessimistic
- Are filled with fear
- Are told with destructive language
- Are discouraging to self and others

The Lesser Life
Is characterized by:
- Fear
- Illness
- Pessimism
- Spiritual emptiness
- Cowardice
- Self-involvement
- A lack of options
- A narrow focus
- Passivity
- A poor sense of humor
- Anxiety and depression
- Purposelessness

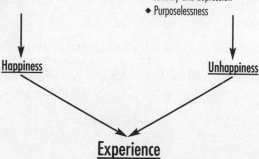

Happiness   **Unhappiness**

Experience

"Do you remember the time you told me I was going sane?" Emily asked.

"You were sitting right there, in that chair. How long ago was that?"

"Three years. Three and a half. That was just before my lumpectomy. Before Bill and I got married. Before Bryan went to college. Back in the day . . ."

She looked wistful, as if remembering the best time of her life.

"You look so much younger," I said. "You must be doing well."

"We all are. Bryan's great. New girlfriend. He's so sweet. Bill just got put on a new account, so he's losing his mind. But he's good."

"How's the health?"

"Great. Oh. Not exactly great, I guess. I've got a tiny little cancerous lesion on my cervix, but it's no biggie. They say they can snip it off in about 20 minutes. Excellent prognosis. Couldn't be better. But let me show you a picture of Bryan. He's on the cross-country team. Is this kid handsome, or what?"

"So you're not worried?"

"I'm not exactly thrilled. But Bill's been so good about it. Bryan, too. Remember what a rock he was, back then?"

What a difference! I was so proud of her.

"So have you learned the meaning of life?" I was being sort of flippant. But not entirely. Not with this woman.

"The meaning of life?" She looked dead serious. "Of course I've learned the meaning of life." She smiled. "The meaning of life is to live."

I've never forgotten that. And I've never forgotten what she said next.

"I think I even know the secret of happiness."

"You do?"

"It's this: Every moment that's ever been, or ever will be, is gone the instant it's begun. So life *is* loss. And the secret of happiness is to learn to love the moment more than you mourn the loss."

She smiled again. That smile! My God, it was a beautiful smile.

I kept seeing it all day long, that smile.

I can see it even now.

All right, you're thinking: How can you end a book on happiness without a happy ending? She's got *cancer*.

Well . . . this *is* a happy ending. This is the one where the heroine lands in a world of hurt, a life much harder than she'd ever thought, struggling and striving, finally settling on not just surviving, and opening herself at last to the pain and grace of love, even as it recedes before her—until, in her despair, suddenly it's there and she smiles, knowing it won't be easy, not caring, knowing this life can't last, not caring, knowing that nothing lasts but love, not caring, smiling, smiling.

This is Emily's story.

And yours.

This *is* happiness: bittersweet, often broken, a poem sometimes left unspoken—full of longing and opportunity missed, made wise by sorrows that never last, a promise to ourselves, from deep in the past. A future with fears that never arrive: This is happiness—this moment, this *now*—this being alive.